Collins

NEW MATHS FRAMEWORKING

Functional Skills

Keith Gordon, Chris Pearce, Trevor Senior

William Collins' dream of knowledge for all began with the publication of his first book in 1819. A self-educated mill worker, he not only enriched millions of lives, but also founded a flourishing publishing house. Today, staying true to this spirit, Collins books are packed with inspiration, innovation and practical expertise. They place you at the centre of a world of possibility and give you exactly what you need to explore it.

Collins. Do more.

Published by Collins
An imprint of HarperCollins*Publishers*
77 – 85 Fulham Palace Road
Hammersmith
London
W6 8JB

Browse the complete Collins catalogue at
www.collinseducation.com

© HarperCollins*Publishers* Limited 2009

10 9 8 7 6

ISBN-13 978 0 00 731843 8

Keith Gordon, Chris Pearce and Trevor Senior assert their moral rights to be identified as the authors of this work

Any educational institution that has purchased one copy of this publication may make unlimited duplicate copies for use exclusively within that institution. Permission does not extend to reproduction, storage within a retrieval system, or transmittal in any form or by any means, electronic, mechanical, photocopying, recording or otherwise, of duplicate copies for loaning, renting or selling to any other institution without the permission of the Publisher.

British Library Cataloguing in Publication Data
A Catalogue record for this publication is available from the British Library

Project managed by Letitia Luff
Edited and proofread by Joan Miller
Cover design, content design and typesetting by Linda Miles, Lodestone Publishing Limited
Illustrations by Jerry Fowler
Production by Therese Webb

Printed by Martins the Printers, Berwick upon Tweed

This book is proudly printed on paper which contains wood from well managed forests, certified in accordance with the rules of the Forest Stewardship Council. For more information about FSC, please visit www.fsc-uk.org

Contents

Introduction   4–7

Activities

⭐ Beginner

Endangered species	8–10
Football	11–14
Paving	15–17
Money matters 1: Pay	18–21
Wales	22–26
Bricklaying patterns	27–31
Deliveries	32–35
Water	36–38
Safe flying over the UK	39–40
Darts	41–43

⭐⭐ Improver

Bridges	44–46
Money matters 2: Tax and national insurance	47–49
Revision planning	50–51
At the gym	52–55
Money matters 3: Loans and APR	56–59
Stickers	60–64
Money matters 4: Savings and AER	65–66
Shuffleboard	67–70
Money matters 5: Mortgages	71–72
Time zones	73–76

⭐⭐⭐ Advanced

Planning a bedroom	77–79
Stopping distances	80–85
Climate change	86–87
Growing, growing, grown…	88–92
Recipes	93–96
Venting gas appliances	97–103
Timetables	104–109
Alcohol	110–113
Garden designer	114–115
Saving energy	116–117

Rich Tasks

Rugby numbers	118–120
Join a group	121–124
Follow that car	125–130
Bike race	131–138
Tile that wall	139–143
Body mass index	144–149
Green travel	150–154
Turn up the volume	155–157
Give us a job	158–162
Populations	163–169

Matching charts

3-year Scheme of Work matching chart	170
Year 9 Scheme of work matching chart	171
Framework matching chart	172–174
Functional Skills checklist	175

Introduction

What do we mean by functional mathematics?

Perhaps your first thought is about mathematics in a real life context. More broadly it means giving student the knowledge and skills they need to use mathematics confidently and effectively in life and work.

What does that mean in practice for you? We want students to recognise when they could use mathematics in a particular situation; to choose a way to tackle a problem; to be confident about applying their knowledge; to use mathematics to provide answers; to interpret and check their results; and to judge how successful they have been. This sounds like a lot! Actually it is not as drastic as it appears at first. Students just need to be given more chances to use the mathematical skills and techniques you are teaching them already.

Why is functional mathematics important?

Just think about these points.
- The Programmes of Study in The National Curriculum 2007 have a section on Key Processes, defined as 'the essential skills and processes in mathematics that students need to learn'. Under the headings of Representing, Analysing, Interpreting and evaluating, and Communicating and reflecting, these skills and processes are listed in some detail.
- The Secondary Mathematics Framework expands these concepts in the section on Mathematical processes and applications, listing learning objectives across Key Stages 3 and 4.
- The new GCSE specifications for first teaching from 2010 require that around 30% of the marks will be awarded for selecting and applying mathematical methods, and around 20% for interpreting and analysing problems and generating strategies to solve them.
- A Functional Mathematics qualification will be a requirement for all students taking a Diploma and there is an expectation that all school students will be entered for Functional Mathematics assessment.

All of these are either explicitly or implicitly about functional mathematics. We could in future be teaching lessons where the objectives are not about learning of new techniques but about helping students learn how to use the techniques they already have in a realistic situation.

Planning for progression

The point to remember is that students can be taught to be confident and reflective users of mathematics and over time we can help them move towards that goal. So what does 'progression' look like when we are talking about functional mathematics? It helps to look at these four factors:
- The **complexity** of the application. Is it a routine or a non-routine problem? Does it require a number of steps to reach a solution? Does it involve extended enquiry?

Introduction

- The **familiarity** of the context. Is the scenario drawn from other subjects or from other aspects of students' lives?
- The **technical demand** of the mathematics required. How advanced are the concepts and procedures needed?
- The degree of **independence** and autonomy of the student. Can the students make decisions and choices for themselves?

Let's think about progression in terms of these four strands.

- At first students can tackle tasks which are easily accessible. It is straight forward for students to see how technical skills they have can be applied in a realistic situation. They may need support and guidance to successfully plan what they will do and carry out the task.
- As students progress and become more competent they will be able to work more independently on problems and tasks in less familiar contexts which have increasing complexity and technical demand.
- Eventually they will progress to tackling complex problems and adapt their knowledge to do so. They will have the ability to select the mathematical tools they need and use them independently.

When you are planning your lessons, think about what stage your students are at. Think too about how you want them to develop as they move through the school.

What will the lessons be like?

Look at the teaching plans in this book. How different are they from 'ordinary' mathematics lessons? One thing you will notice is that the learning objectives are not about acquiring a mathematical skill, they are about such things as recognising what mathematical tools might be useful or drawing conclusions from an investigation. You will also see that the starting point is something drawn from real life. Frequently students are given opportunities to work together and present their findings to the rest of the class, to encourage them to talk about mathematics and experience it as a group activity. Often, students are given opportunities to make decisions abut what they want to do and to make appropriate plans.

Students welcome the opportunity to do non-routine activities, to work in groups and to tackle investigational tasks. We kept this in mind when we were writing these teaching plans and we hope that your students will find the activities in the Pupil Book varied and interesting. We also hope you will enjoy teaching them!

The activities in this book

These lessons are designed to be a flexible resource that can be used as part of your Scheme of Work for teaching mathematics in KS3 and KS4. Your decision on when to use the activities will depend upon the ability of your students and their stage of development. We have provided several charts at the back of this Teacher Pack to help you decide when to use the activities:

- A matching chart to the New Maths Frameworking 3-year Scheme of Work based on when students will have picked up the mathematical techniques they need to tackle them.

Introduction

- A matching chart to topics in Year 9 to prepare students for the new GCSE in 2010 and fill the gap left by the demise of SATs.
- A chart showing which Strand or Strands of mathematics each activity uses, and the mathematical techniques they need to tackle them.

To avoid confusion with KS3 Levels and KS4 Grades, we have used a star rating to show how challenging a task is.

- ★ **One star** indicates a task that can be tackled using a straightforward approach in a context that will be familiar. Students can be given support from the teacher if they find it difficult to make progress independently.
- ★★ **Two stars** indicate a task where the approach to take will be less obvious. The context will perhaps be less familiar. The technical demand may be greater and students can be encouraged to be more autonomous.
- ★★★ **Three stars** indicate a multi-step problem or a chance to make a more extended enquiry. There will be opportunities for the use of more sophisticated techniques in a non-routine manner. Students can be expected to work independently in planning and carrying out activities.

Of course, you can modify an activity to suit the abilities of the students and we have tried to indicate how you can do that. For example, you could make a one star task more demanding by encouraging greater independence from the students. The objectives given for each task relate to the development of functional skills so that these can be made explicit for students and they can make assessments of their own progression.

Some of the tasks would benefit from access to ICT resources. We know that in some schools it is difficult to get access to such resources and so we have tried to ensure that tasks can still be profitably carried out where resources are limited.

Assessing Pupils' Progress (APP)

The work students produce when carrying out these Functional Maths activities can support APP, especially for Using and applying mathematics. To help you gather evidence we have referenced which assessment criteria each activity could provide for.

Personal, Learning and Thinking Skills (PLTS)

One of the requirements of the National Curriculum is the development of students' PLTS. We think these are closely related to functional mathematics. For example, deciding on the appropriate mathematical tools to use requires creative thinking; evaluating the success of a particular approach requires reflective learning; and so on. Because of this we have included references to PLTS for each activity.

Introduction

Practical questions

How do I know that the lessons will be successful?

Be brave; try it out and see what happens! Teachers who try this sort of activity for the first time are often surprised by how well they turn out. Your students will appreciate the opportunity to work on these activities. Why not get some feedback from them afterwards?

When is the best time to do them?

This is an interesting question. For example, if a task involves students applying their knowledge of symmetry should they do it just after they have been taught a unit on symmetry? It may be better to do it a month or two later, to see if they can recall what they did when the topic is no longer fresh in their minds. Then the task of "choosing the appropriate mathematical tools" becomes a more realistic one and closer to the situation students are likely to experience in life outside school.

What if the students do not do what I expect them to do?

It can be hard to "let go" and not tell students what to do, particularly if you think that a student is using an inefficient or inappropriate technique. However if students are going to learn to be effective and confident users of mathematics, being able to make mistakes and learn from them is an important part of the process.

My Scheme of Work is already full. How can I fit this in as well?

Do you think that they have too much to teach and too little time in which to teach it? Try to think "instead of" rather than "as well as". Lessons that focus on developing the ability of students to use and apply their mathematics are often the best way to foster real understanding. See if you can find some lessons in your Scheme of Work that could be replaced by an activity in this book.

How long will should each activity take?

Try not to not to rush through these tasks and resist the temptation to hurry things along if progress seems slow. The time students need to complete these activities will vary according to their level of expertise: try to give them the time they need.

A final thought

We know that students will respond positively to lessons which they find interesting and enjoyable. We hope that the resources in this book will help you deliver lessons which are varied in content, where mathematics is employed for a real purpose and where students have the opportunity to work with others on an interesting problem; and that in consequence they will learn more effectively.

Endangered species

Context
- The activity is about reading information from tables and charts and accessing key data.
- It is also about interpreting the information and presenting it in a variety of forms.

Lesson plan

Starter
- Ensure that students understand what the term **endangered species** means.
- Point out that all the information given in the table is in **imperial** measurements and that, for example, **lbs** means **pounds**. Explain that, when we are researching information, it is not always expressed in the units we are used to.
- Ask students to study the table of information.
- Ask the students to cover up the table and then recall as many facts as they can.
- Now allow students to look at the table again to see what they missed.
- Ask students to answer the warm-up questions.

Main activity
- The three tasks do not have to be done in the order in which they are presented.
- Before students start Task 1, point out that there may be several correct answers and that some data may be missing, so they have to make decisions or else leave out some animals from their lists. The table is provided on Worksheet: Endangered species so students can cut along rows to rearrange if desired.
- Point out that all the animals on the list are **mammals**. However, not all endangered species are mammals.
- There is probably no link between population and lifespan of animals, but the discussion will be interesting.
- When they have completed Task 1, the students should discuss their findings and try to justify the order they have chosen.
- There is plenty of information, available from many sources, for Task 2 but sometimes it will be contradictory, depending on when it was written or who wrote it.
- The important aspect of this task is that students learn how to collate information and present it in different ways. It could be undertaken partly as a homework.
- Task 3 is simply a series of questions, some of which are related to information in the table and others that are freestanding but related to the same topic.
- You may wish to extend the list of questions or link this task to Task 2, so that students present their own questions and answers for other endangered species.

Learning objectives

Representing: decide how to represent the problem to make it easier to solve using mathematics

Analysing: use appropriate mathematical procedures

Interpreting: interpret results and solutions and make a generalisation about them

Performing: use a range of mathematics to find solutions

APP: evidence for Using and applying mathematics, Numbers and the number system

PLTS: develops Effective participators, Independent enquirers

Cross-curricular links: ICT, Science, Geography

Underpinning maths:
measures
extracting information from tables, diagrams and charts
collect and record data and organise and represent information in different ways

Resources
Pupil Book page 8
reference texts
internet access
Worksheet: Endangered species

Beginner

Plenary
- This part of the activity should be about bringing the different results together for the various tasks.
- A group of students could present their findings from Task 2.

Extension work (open-ended)
- Ask students to consider how this activity can be considered as mathematical.
- This extension work could involve further work on Task 2.
- Ask students to present their findings in different ways. They might use tables, graphs, bar charts or pie charts.
- Ask students to consider other facts apart from population, size and lifespan.
- All the animals listed in the table are mammals. Students could use various sources of information, including internet searches, to find out about other endangered species including non-mammals.

Outcomes
- Students will have had opportunities to identify and obtain information to tackle a problem.
- Students will have had opportunities to use mathematics to investigate practical problems.
- Students will have had opportunities to interpret and communicate information and draw simple conclusions, giving explanations.

Answers

Warm-up questions

1. 20–40 years
2. Longer
3. Approximately 42 000
4. Heavier
5. Male

Task 3

1. Up to 33 metres
2. 182 kg
3. 2%
4. 2 grams
5. 25 000
6. 1.6%

© HarperCollins*Publishers* 2009

 *Beginner*

Worksheet: Endangered species

Animal	Population	Size	Lifespan
Bat	Some bat populations are counted in millions. Others are extremely low or declining.	Large bats can have a wingspan of 6 feet. Small bats can be less than an inch long.	Most bats live longer than most mammals of the same size. The longest known lifespan of a bat in the wild is about 30–40 years.
Grizzly bear	In 1950 there were about 50 000 grizzly bears in North America. Now there are about 1000 remaining, in five separate populations. In Alaska, there are over 30 000 grizzly bears.	**Height:** about $3-3\frac{1}{2}$ feet at shoulders **Length:** 6–7 feet **Adult weight:** male 300–850 lbs; female 200–450 lbs	20–25 years
Whale	Varies with each species.	**Length:** varies, up to 110 feet **Weight:** varies, up to 150 tons	Whales normally live 20–40 years but they can live up to 80 years.
Lion	The lion population in Africa has reduced by half since the early 1950s. Today, fewer than 21 000 remain in all of Africa.	**Height:** males reach 4 feet, females are smaller **Length:** males reach 5-8 feet, females are smaller **Weight:** males reach 330–500 lbs, females weigh less	13 years, although they may live longer in captivity
Chimpanzee	An estimated 100 000 to 200 000 chimpanzees live in the wild.	**Height:** approximately 4 feet **Weight:** males 90–120 lbs, females 60–110 lbs	Chimpanzees rarely live past the age of 50 in the wild, but have been known to reach the age of 60 in captivity.

Football

Context
- This context will be familiar to nearly all students and should provide some lively discussion, depending on football loyalties.
- The first two tasks are basically numerical but Task 3 is an investigation in which students can develop process skills.

Lesson plan

Starter
- Ask students how the football league in England is structured. They will almost certainly know that, in England, there are four principal leagues: the Premiership, the Championship, League 1 and League 2. Below this are various semi-professional leagues that feed into the conference league, from which a team is promoted each year to League 2. Below the semi-professional leagues is a hierarchy of amateur leagues, with local pub teams probably playing in the lowest of these. Successful teams can be promoted up the leagues while unsuccessful teams are relegated down the leagues.
- Establish the structure and how teams score points within the league. In England the rule is 3 points for a win, 1 for a draw and none for a loss.
- Ask students if they know how the FA cup is organised. This is a knockout competition with several preliminary rounds leading to a final at Wembley. The names of teams are drawn from a 'hat'. This means that teams from different leagues can play against each other; so-called 'non-league' teams are often drawn against premiership teams, leading to the term 'giant-killers'.

Main activity
- The starter discussion will have provided enough information for students to tackle Task 1 and then Task 2 without any further introduction.
- Students should do these two tasks before Task 3, which is an investigation aimed at developing process skills, is introduced.
- A good introduction is to use a score from a recent high-profile game, such as an important Premiership or European Championships league game. This needs to have a fairly high score, such as 3–2.
- Ask students what the half-time score was. Football fans in the class will know this but, just in case, have the information available. Suppose it was 2–0, for example.
- Ask them what other scores there could have been at half-time.
- Write students' suggestions on the board. It is likely that these will be quite random. Write them as students suggest them so that they appear to be random on the board.

Learning objectives

Representing: decide how to represent the problem to make it easier to solve using mathematics

Analysing: establish a pattern or relationship and then change the variables to see how this changes the results

Interpreting: test generalisations and draw conclusions from the mathematical analysis

Performing: analyse the situation or problem and decide which is the appropriate mathematical method needed to tackle it

APP: evidence for using and applying mathematics, Algebra, Calculating

PLTS: develops Independent enquirers

Cross-curricular links: ICT, PE

Underpinning maths:
basic numeracy
negative numbers
powers
basic algebra

Resources
Pupil Book page 11
computers
spreadsheet program (optional)
Worksheet: Football

★ *Beginner*

- There are 12 possible half-time scores for a final score of 3–2, so it may take some time for students to suggest all of them and some may be missed.
- Ask if there is any way we can be sure to get all scores. Someone may suggest writing the scores in an organised way. If not, suggest this.
- Start with a home score of zero. The potential half-time scores are therefore 0–0, 0–1 and 0–2.
- Repeat with a home score of 1, giving potential half-time scores of 1–0, 1–1 and 1–2.
- Repeat with home scores of 2 and 3 to give all 12 scores.
- These should be written in an organised way on the board.

> 0–0 1–0 2–0 3–0
> 0–1 1–1 2–1 3–1
> 0–2 1–2 2–2 3–2

- Now ask students to pick a final score and write down all the potential half-time scores.
- After they have done this, collect together some results; for example, 2–1 has 6 possible half-time scores, 4–5 has 30 potential half-time scores. Again, take these quite randomly.
- It is unlikely that students will spot the rule so now ask if there is any better way of showing the results. Someone may suggest a table.
- Before filling in the table, ask students to suggest a logical manner for recording the numbers, to help them spot any patterns. For example, they may suggest starting with 0–0 and building up from there.
- Start to fill in the table. It may be appropriate to use a spreadsheet for this.

Home team	Away team	Number of possible half-time scores
0	0	1
0	1	2
0	2	3
1	0	2
1	1	4
1	2	6

- Ask students to copy the table and then to add extra results to it. Alternatively the table is provided on Worksheet: Football.
- After a while, ask them if they can spot a rule.
- Initially they may say that for a score of nil-'something' the number of possible half-time scores is one more than the 'something', or that the answer for 0–2 is the same as 2–0.
- Encourage students to record any rules they see.
- Ask for a more general rule. **Hint:** it is something to do with multiplication.
- They will probably say that it is 'one more than the home score multiplied by one more than the away score'.
- Now explain that they are going to put this into a mathematical rule.
- Students may have met basic algebra; if not, suggest that the home team's score is called *h* and the away team's score is called *a*.

© HarperCollins*Publishers* 2009

Beginner

- Ask students to express the rule in an algebraic form, for example, '*h* + 1 x *a* + 1'.
- Make sure that students understand the need for brackets: (*h* + 1)(*a* + 1).
- Once the algebraic rule has been established make sure students test their rule with a new example, or test it with the score used when the task was introduced.

Plenary

Go through with students the process skills needed in an investigation:
- breaking down the problem into simple cases (0–0, 0–1, etc.)
- working logically (0–0, 0–1, 0–2, etc.)
- recording results in a table
- looking for patterns
- writing down generalisations
- testing generalisations
- extending results
- using algebra to write down a general rule.

Outcomes

Students will have used process skills to investigate a simple real context problem.

Answers

Task 1

1   760

2   (+)36

3   23

4   Overall there must be the same number of goals scored as goals scored against.

5   15

6   114

7   a   38   b   26 wins and 12 draws

8   8 draws, 1 loss

9   3 wins, 2 draws, 33 losses; 2 wins, 5 draws, 31 losses; 1 wins, 8 draws, 29 losses; 0 wins, 11 draws and 27 losses.

10   a T   b F   c F   d T (based on a line of best fit)

Task 2

1 256   **2** 506   **3** 1024   **4** 2^n

Task 3

See the notes above for the main activity: number of possible half-time scores for a final score of *h*–*a* is (*h* + 1)(*a* + 1).

Beginner

Worksheet: Football

Home team	Away team	Number of possible half-time scores
0	0	1
0	1	2
0	2	3
1	0	2
1	1	4
1	2	6

Paving

Context
- The activity is about making choices when using tessellations, planning areas and making costings.

Lesson plan
Starter
- Display a selection of shapes, as shown in the Pupil Book.

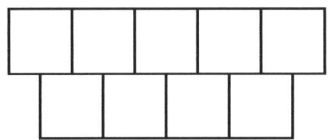
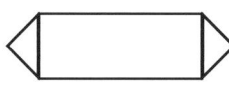

- Build up some tessellations, using shapes from the sheet.
- Now ask students to use some of these shapes to make their own tessellations on squared paper.

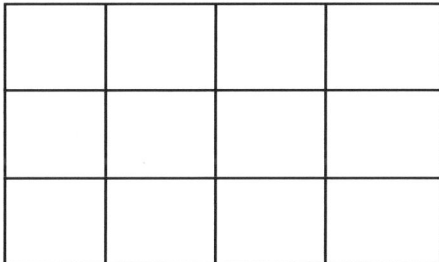

- Explain to the students that they will be using these shapes to design a paved area for a garden.

Main activity
- Ask the students to answer the warm-up questions.
- Now look together at Task 1.
- Explain that there are two ways of laying out the slabs but one is more practical than the other.
- Show students a rectangle, 12 cm long and 6 cm wide, with 12 smaller rectangles, 3 cm long and 2 cm wide. Explain or demonstrate how the small rectangles fit into the large rectangle.

- Check that students know that 60 metres is 6000 cm and that 10 metres is 1000 cm.
- Ask students to complete Task 1 and Task 2.
- Now go through the price lists with the students, explaining the deals for bulk buying.
- Ask students to complete Task 3. Accept a selection of answers to check that the students have understood the problem.

Learning objectives

Representing: recognise that a real-life problem can be solved using appropriate mathematics; decide how to represent the problem to make it easier to solve using mathematics

Analysing: analyse a pattern or a relationship, using appropriate techniques

Interpreting: interpret results and solutions and make a generalisation about them; check that a conclusion is appropriate and accurate in the context of the original problem

Performing: check work and methods when tackling a problem and decide if a different approach may be more effective; give a solution to a practical problem, even if it is not within a familiar context, and make sure the solution is presented in a clear and understandable way

APP: evidence for Using and applying mathematics, Shape, space and measures

PLTS: develops Creative thinkers, Independent enquirers

Cross-curricular links: ICT

© HarperCollins*Publishers* 2009

Beginner

- For Task 4 and Task 5 students will need to use centimetre-squared paper and produce scale drawings and scale models of the paving slabs.
- Task 5, the extension work, is very open-ended. If necessary, it could be made more structured by giving dimensions and restricting the shapes to those already used in earlier tasks. Alternatively, students could use internet searches to find different shapes of slab and design their own patterns.

Plenary
- Go over the students' answers as a class.
- List and discuss the problems that arose as they were designing their gardens.

Outcomes
- Students will have made sure the solution is presented in a clear and understandable way.
- Students will have used mathematics to gain insight into a real-life problem.

Underpinning maths:
scale drawing
tessellations
area
money problems in context

Resources
Pupil Book page 14
squared paper
graph paper
internet access
Worksheet: Paving

Answers

Warm-up questions

1. 100
2. 120 cm
3. £258
4. £258 + £378 = £636
5. 600 m²
6. £11
7. 25
8. 20
9. 5 with £10 left over
10. 20 of each

Worksheet: Paving

Beginner

Money matters 1: Pay

Context
- This is the first of five activities that deal with the money issues that students will meet during their lifetimes. They cover basic pay (here), tax and national insurance (page 47), loans (page 56), savings (page 65) and mortgages (page 71).
- The mathematics involved is basic numeracy and use of calculators is recommended.

Lesson plan

Starter
- Depending on the ability level of the class, students could practise some basic numeracy skills.
- Doubling amounts such as £3.23 and £4.75 and using the concept of **one and a half** or **one and a quarter** on simple amounts such as £2.00 or £4.40 would give students some idea of the mathematics involved in the tasks; however, the class may use calculators.

Main activity
- Discuss with students what they know about being paid for work. It is likely that some of them have part-time jobs.
- Establish the difference between wage-earners and salaried staff.
- Ask students if they know about the minimum wage. Discuss what this means. The rates established on 1 October 2008 are given in the Pupil Book. These may have changed; students could look up the latest rates on the internet.
- It may be worth discussing the normally accepted wage that is regarded as the **poverty threshold** for a family. This was £7 per hour in 2007. Again, students could find out more by trying an internet search.
- Ask students if they know the normal number of hours a worker will typically work in a week. This is about 40, usually a few hours less for salaried staff.
- Ask students to suggest an hourly wage and a number of hours worked.
- Ask them how they would calculate typical earnings, using the figures they have suggested.
- It may be worth pointing out that this is the **gross earnings** figure and it is not necessarily what the person takes home.
- Ask students if they know why **gross earnings** and **take-home pay** are different. (Tax and national insurance are the main deductions but other things can be taken off, such as pension payments.) All tables for this activity are reproduced on Worksheet: Pay.
- Before they start Task 1, work through a couple of examples, filling in some rows from the table. Good starting points would be Betty, Eddy and Ian.

Learning objectives

Representing: recognise that a real-life problem can be solved using appropriate mathematics; decide how to represent the problem to make it easier to solve using mathematics

Analysing: find a result or solution to the original problem

Interpreting: check that a conclusion is appropriate and accurate in the context of the original problem

Performing: use mathematical skills and knowledge to make progress on a problem, even if it does not use a routine mathematical procedure; give a solution to a practical problem, even if it is not within a familiar context, and make sure the solution is presented in a clear and understandable way

APP: evidence for Calculating

PLTS: develops Independent enquirers, Effective participators

Cross-curricular links: ICT

Underpinning maths: numeracy fractions and decimals

Beginner

Resources
Pupil Book page 16
internet access
Worksheet: Pay

- Ask students to complete Task 1.
- Ask students what would happen if someone worked longer than the required hours.
- Establish the principle of **overtime** and the fact that the rates of pay for this are typically higher than for the normal working week.
- Refer to colloquial terms such as **time-and-a-half** and **double-time**, which mean the hourly rate is multiplied by 1.5 and 2 respectively for overtime hours.
- Before they start Task 2, work through a couple of examples, filling in some rows from the table. Good starting points would be Belinda, Francis and Henry.
- Ask students to complete Task 2.
- The idea of an annual salary paid monthly will already have been established.
- Students should find Task 3 straightforward.

Plenary

- Discuss the concepts and mathematics used.
- In reality many things also affect weekly earnings. Time may be deducted for a worker being late.
- Some workers, particularly those on production lines or doing repetitive tasks, are on **piece-work**, which means they get paid a basic rate and get more money depending on how many of the items they produce.
- Some occupations, such as waiting, can have tips included as part of the basic wage.

Outcomes

- Students will have had the opportunity to use basic numeracy in a real-life situation.

Answers

Task 1

Aftab: £252; Betty: £229.20; Colin: £513; Deidre: £105.90; Eddy: 35 hours; Frank: 40 hours; Gus: £2.75 per hour; Hinna: £9.80 per hour; Ian: 18–21 years old; Jemima: 16 or 17 years old

Task 2

Alf, £410; Belinda, £272.18; Chas, £552; Dave £158.85; Edith, 5 hours; Francis, 4 hours; Gaynor, £3.20 per hour; Henry, £9 per hour; Iris, 18-21 years old; Jack, 16 or 17 years old.

Task 3

Pete: £30 000; Quinlan: £40 200; Rosie: £1875; Sue: £6210, £50 160

Extension questions

1   £598.50

2   £277.85

3   £7.50

4   18–21 years old

5   £213.84

© HarperCollins*Publishers* 2009

Beginner

Worksheet: Pay

Task 1

Name	Age	Hours	Wage per hour	Total weekly wages
Aftab	30	35	£7.20	
Betty	25	40	MW	
Colin	42	38	£13.50	
Diedre	17	30	MW	
Eddy	28		£8.75	£306.25
Frank	21		MW	£190.80
Gus	15	8		£22.00
Hinna	25	37.5		£367.50
Ian		36	MW	£171.72
Jemima		20	MW	£70.60

Task 2

Name	Age	Basic hours	Overtime hours	Basic wage per hour	Overtime rate	Total wages
Alf	32	35	10	£8.20	1.5 x	
Belinda	27	40	6	MW	1.25 x	
Chas	42	36	8	£11.50	1.5 x	
Dave	17	35	5	MW	2 x	
Edith	29	40		£8.75	1.4 x	£411.25
Francis	20	35		MW	1.5 x	£195.57
Gaynor	14	10	2		1.5 x	£41.60
Henry	26	40	6		1.25 x	£427.50
Iris		38	8	MW	1.5 x	£238.50
Jack		35	10	MW	1.25 x	£167.68

© HarperCollins*Publishers* 2009

Worksheet: Pay

Task 3

Name	Monthly salary	Annual salary
Pete	£2500	
Quinlan	£3350	
Rosie		£22 500
Sue		£74 520
Teresa	£4180	

Wales

Context
- This activity is about reading information from tables and charts and accessing key data.
- It is also about interpreting information and presenting it in a variety of forms.

Lesson plan

Starter
- Look at the Data sheet: Wales and ask students to give you facts from the graphs. For example, a greater percentage of 10–15-year-olds than other age groups can speak Welsh.
- Ask students to comment on any trends they can see, for example:
  - The proportion of people living in Wales who were born in Wales is falling.
  - The proportion who can speak Welsh was falling but is starting to rise.
- Look at the name of the longest village. Let students try to say it!

Main activity
- Use Tasks 1 and 2 to test whether the students can derive information when other information is also given.
- Check that students know how to work out a percentage of a quantity:
  - using a build-up method, for example, 19% = 10% + 10% − 1%
  - or using a formal method, for example,
    19% of 3 000 000 = $\frac{19}{100} \times 3\,000\,000$.
- Point out that when graphs show percentages of age groups, they could be misleading as the number in each age group might be different; for example, people aged 75 and over may be a much bigger or much smaller group than people aged 65–74.
- Students can now complete Tasks 1 and 2.
- Recall the eight-point compass and bearings.

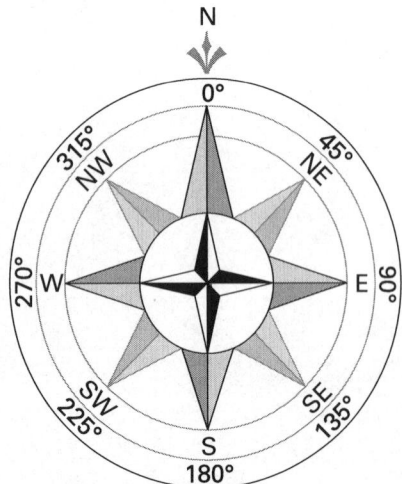

- Students can now complete Task 3.

Learning objectives

Representing: decide which methods to use to make progress with the solution

Analysing: use appropriate mathematical procedures

Interpreting: test generalisations and draw conclusions from the mathematical analysis

Performing: use mathematical skills and knowledge to make progress on a real-life problem, even if the situation described is not within a familiar context

APP: evidence for Using and applying mathematics, Handling data

PLTS: develops Effective participators, Team workers

Cross-curricular links: ICT, Geography

Underpinning maths:
percentages
proportions
tally charts
bar charts
probability
eight-point compass
three-figure bearings

Resources
Pupil Book page 20
internet access
Data sheet: Wales

© HarperCollins Publishers 2009

Beginner

Plenary
- Ask students to give you some facts about Wales that have not been used in the tasks. They could carry out internet searches or use reference books and atlases for this.

Extension work
- Task 3 could be used to introduce three-figure bearings. For example, east = 090°, south-west = 225°.
- Ask students to repeat Task 3, giving their answers as three-figure bearings.

Outcomes
- Students will have extracted information from tables and graphs.
- Students will have used an eight-point compass and bearings.

Answers

Task 1

1 80%

2 1901

3 730 miles

4 3600 feet

5 10–15 year olds

6 8

7 58.5 °C

8 Any answer between 1981 and 1991

9 5183 square kilometres (Accept 5100–5200)

10 570 000

Task 2

1.

Letter	Tally	Frequency
A	III	3
G	⊦⊦⊦ II	7
L	⊦⊦⊦ ⊦⊦⊦ I	11
O	⊦⊦⊦ I	6
W	IIII	4
Y	⊦⊦⊦ I	6
Other	⊦⊦⊦ ⊦⊦⊦ ⊦⊦⊦ ⊦⊦⊦ I	21

© HarperCollins*Publishers* 2009

 *Beginner*

2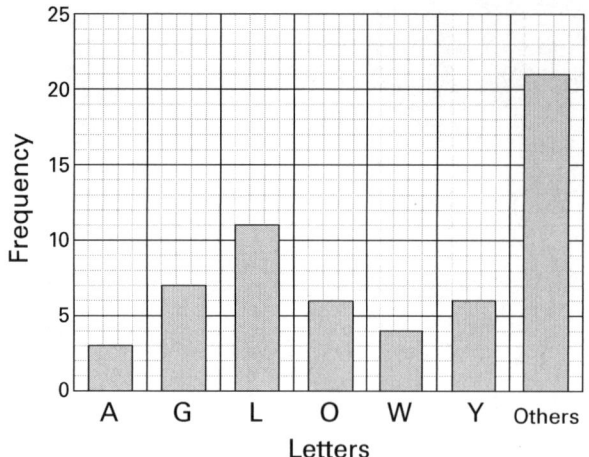

3 a L   b $\frac{7}{58}$ c $\frac{51}{58}$

Task 3

1 Cardiff is east of Swansea.

2 Tywyn is north of Aberystwyth

3 Cardigan is north-east of Fishguard

4 Bangor is south-east of Holyhead

5 Swansea is south-west of Brecon

6 Holyhead is west of Colwyn Bay

Extension work

1 090°

2 000° or 360°

3 045°

4 135°

5 225°

6 270°

Beginner

Data sheet: Wales

Population:

- approximately **3 million**
- **19%** of population aged **under 16**
- 75% of people living in Wales in 2001 were **born in Wales**.
- 20% of people living in Wales in 2001 were **born in England**.
- 5% of people living in Wales in 2001 were born **in other UK countries or countries outside the UK.**

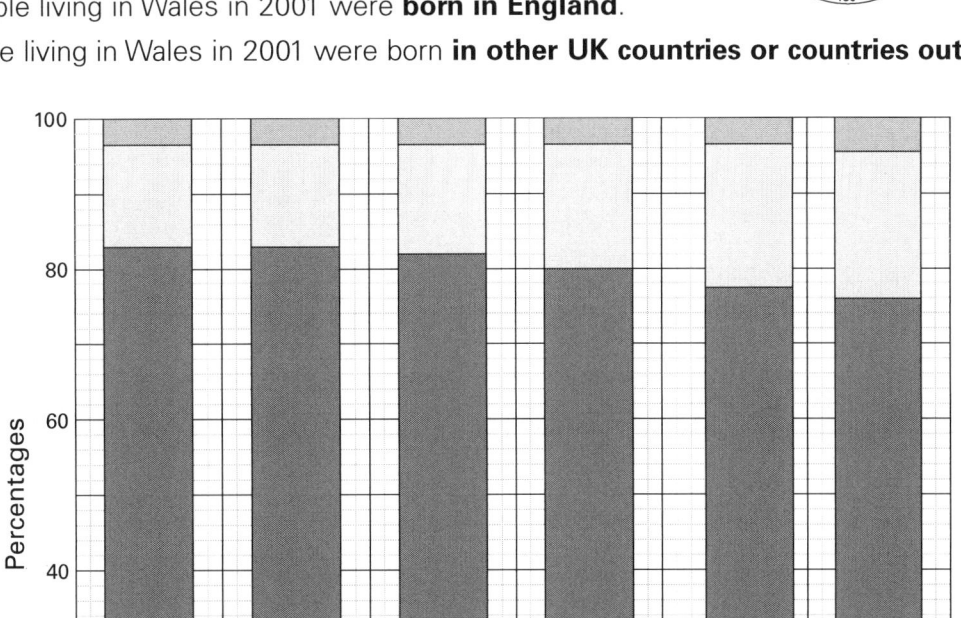

People living in Wales: by country of birth

- **21%** of the population of Wales said they could speak Welsh **in 2001**.
- More schools are **now teaching Welsh**.

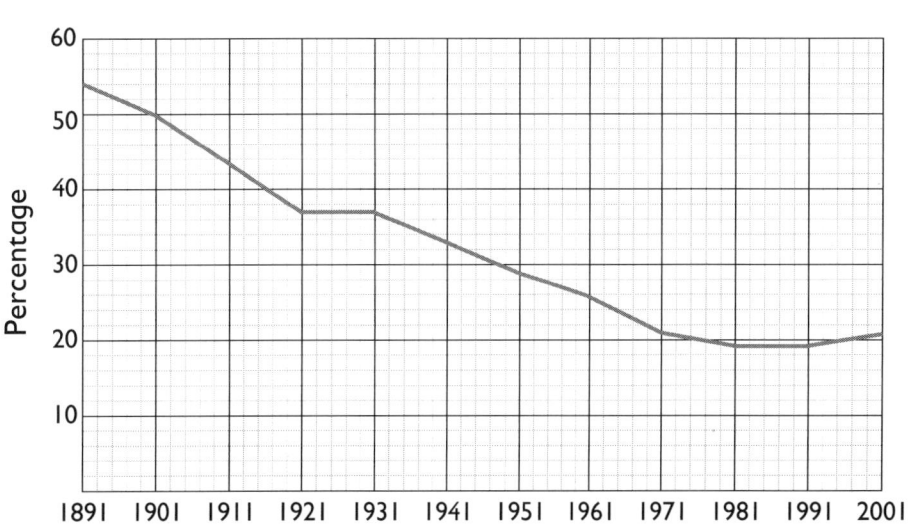

Proportion of people aged 3 and over able to speak Welsh

© HarperCollins*Publishers* 2009

★ *Beginner*

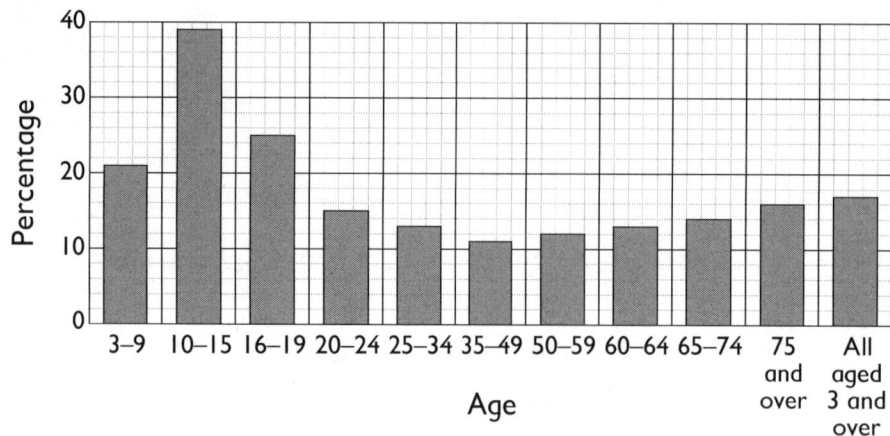

Ability to speak, read and write Welsh: by age, April 2001

- The village with the **longest name** in Wales is in Anglesey and is
  LLANFAIRPWLLGWYNGYLLGOGERYCHWYNDROBWYLLLLANTYSILIOGOGOGOCH
- It has **58 letters**, or 51 in the Welsh alphabet, in which ch and ll count as single letters.
- Wales has an **area** of **20 732 square kilometres** (about **8000 square miles**).
- 25% of Wales is either **National Park** or an **Area of outstanding natural beauty**.
- The **capital** of Wales is **Cardiff**.
- There are **732 miles** of **coastline**.
- **Snowdon**, at **3560 feet**, is the **highest mountain** in Wales and higher than England's highest peak.
- One in five **Welsh MPs** are **women**.
- The **coldest day** in Wales was **21 January 1940**, when the temperature was **−23.3 °C** in Rhayder, Powys.
- The **warmest day** in Wales was **2 August 1990**, when the temperature was **35.2 °C** in Hawarden Bridge, Clwyd.

Table for Task 2

Letter	Tally	Frequency
A		
G		
L		
O		
W		
Y		
Others		

Bricklaying patterns

Context
- This activity is primarily about **symmetry**. However, it can also be used to introduce some ideas about **infinity** and **topology**. Much of the mathematics and concepts will be covered in the starter and the main lesson activity.

Lesson plan
Starter
- Give each student a strip of paper about 20 cm long by 2 cm wide.

- Ask students each to look at their strip and say how many **sides** it has.
- Ask how many **edges** it has. Ask how many **faces** it has.
- Ask students if they think that a cut-out shape can have fewer sides, fewer edges or fewer faces.
- A cut-out triangle has three sides and three edges, but still has two faces.
- Ask them to make a twist in the paper rectangle.

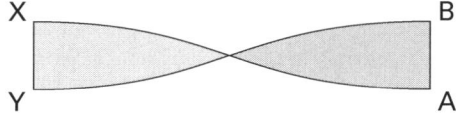

- Now ask them to hold the paper so that the two ends can be glued or taped together. Corner B should join to corner X and corner A should join to corner Y.

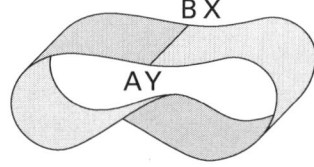

- What they have made is a Möbius strip, which has the property of having only one side and one edge.
- Ask students to mark a starting point, then trace their finger along the edge. They will come back to the same point, without taking their finger off the edge.
- Ask them to draw a line along the centre of one side and keep the line going. They will eventually get back to where they started without changing sides. They should keep their strips for the plenary.
- Tell students that what they have been doing is connected with a branch of mathematics called **topology**, which is the study of shapes in two and three dimensions. (The map of the London Underground is the most famous example of a topological map.

Learning objectives
Representing: recognise that a real-life problem can be solved using appropriate mathematics

Performing: use your mathematical skills and knowledge to make progress on a real-life problem, even if the situation described is not within a familiar context; give a solution to a practical problem, even if it is not within a familiar context and make sure the solution is presented in a clear and understandable way; use a range of mathematics to find solutions

APP: evidence for Shape, space and measure

PLTS: develops Independent enquirers, Creative thinkers

Cross-curricular links: ICT, Art, History

Underpinning maths:
symmetry

© HarperCollins*Publishers* 2009

 *Beginner*

It shows all the stations and lines but does this with smooth curves and lines to replace the actual twists and bends of the underground system.)
- A practical application of the Möbius strip is in a conveyor belt with a twist in it. Wear and tear is even on both sides so these conveyor belts last twice as long as those without twists.
- As an added point of interest, there is a rollercoaster ride at Blackpool pleasure beach called the *Grand National* that is a Möbius strip. Students could use an internet search to find out more about it.

Main activity

- Discuss the idea of the infinite plane with students.
- Distribute Worksheet: Bricklaying patterns to each student.
- Explain that the first activity is a wordsearch with the names of 13 animals hidden in it.
- Start with an easy one – CAT (backwards in fourth row)
- Now ask for DOG. This is not easy to spot so explain that the words can run from one side of the grid to the other or, if it easier to see, explain that the grid is repeated in all directions.
- Show students the grid repeated (see Resource sheet: Bricklaying patterns) on an OHP or Interactive Whiteboard.
- DOG can now be seen backwards on the top row. Do a couple more (Say CAMEL and COLT).
- Take away the repeating grid then ask students to find the rest which are, including those already mentioned, Camel, Carp, Cat, Clam, Colt, Dog, Goat, Loon, Onyx, Orca, Pig, Rhea, Tapir.
- Now look at the exercise in the Pupil Book.
- Talk through the two examples shown and the symmetries of the Stretcher bond arrangement.
- Copies of the paving pattern diagrams and tracing paper are useful for this work.
- Work through Task 1 to make sure students understand what to do.
- The symmetries of Flemish bond are:
  - a vertical line of symmetry through the centre of any brick (footer or header)
  - a horizontal line of symmetry through the centre of any line of bricks
  - rotational symmetry of order 2 through the centre of any brick
  - rotational symmetry of order 2 through a point halfway between the base of one header and the top of the adjacent header on the row below.
- Ask students to do tasks 2 and 3. A worksheet is provided for this.

Plenary

- Ask students to revisit their Möbius strips. Ask:
  - 'What happens when something is cut in half?'
  - 'How many pieces do you get?'
- Distribute scissors and ask students to cut their Möbius strips down the middle, along the line drawn earlier.
- Ask them to say what happens.

Resources
Pupil Book page 23
prepared strips of paper about 20 cm by 2 cm
glue or sticky tape
tracing paper
scissors
internet access
Resource sheet: Bricklaying patterns
Worksheet: Bricklaying patterns

© HarperCollins*Publishers* 2009

Beginner ⭐

Outcomes
- Students will understand the concept of infinity.
- Students will have used line and rotational symmetry.

Answers

Task 1

See the main lesson activity.

Task 2

Stack bond has:
- vertical lines of symmetry through the joins or the centres of any bricks
- horizontal lines of symmetry through the joins or the centres of any bricks
- rotational symmetry order 2 through the centres of bricks and the centres of any edge.

English bond has:
- vertical line symmetry through the centre of any brick
- horizontal line symmetry through the centre of any row of bricks
- rotational symmetry order 2 through the centre of any brick or the centre of the vertical edge of any stretcher.

English cross bond has:
- vertical line symmetry through the centre of any brick
- horizontal line symmetry through the centre of any row of bricks
- rotational symmetry of order 2 through the centre of any stretcher and the centre of any vertical join of 2 headers.

Monk bond has:
- vertical line symmetry through the centre of any header and the vertical join of any two stretchers
- horizontal line symmetry through the centre of any row of bricks
- rotational symmetry order 2 through the centre of any header and the centre of any vertical join of 2 stretchers.

Task 3

Herringbone has rotational symmetry order 2 through the centre of the join where two vertical or horizontal bricks touch.

Basketweave has vertical and horizontal line symmetry through the join of any two adjacent horizontal or vertical bricks and rotational symmetry order 2 about the centre of the join of any two adjacent horizontal or vertical bricks.

Pinwheel has rotational symmetry order 4 through the centre of the small centre square.

De laRobia weave has vertical and horizontal symmetry through the centre of any brick and rotational symmetry order 2 through the centre of any brick.

© HarperCollins*Publishers* 2009

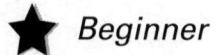
Beginner

Resource sheet: Bricklaying patterns

Wordsearch

E	S	P	G	O	D	E	S	P	G	O	D	E	S	P	G	O
T	A	O	C	O	L	T	A	O	C	O	L	T	A	O	C	O
T	S	R	N	L	A	T	S	R	N	L	A	T	S	R	N	L
T	A	C	C	Y	A	T	A	C	C	Y	A	T	A	C	C	Y
M	T	A	P	R	X	M	T	A	P	R	X	M	T	A	P	R
I	M	R	I	N	H	I	M	R	I	N	H	I	M	R	I	N
E	S	P	G	O	D	E	S	P	G	O	D	E	S	P	G	O
T	A	O	C	O	L	T	A	O	C	O	L	T	A	O	C	O
T	S	R	N	L	A	T	S	R	N	L	A	T	S	R	N	L
T	A	C	C	Y	A	T	A	C	C	Y	A	T	A	C	C	Y
M	T	A	P	R	X	M	T	A	P	R	X	M	T	A	P	R
I	M	R	I	N	H	I	M	R	I	N	H	I	M	R	I	N
E	S	P	G	O	D	E	S	P	G	O	D	E	S	P	G	O
T	A	O	C	O	L	T	A	O	C	O	L	T	A	O	C	O
T	S	R	N	L	A	T	S	R	N	L	A	T	S	R	N	L
T	A	C	C	Y	A	T	A	C	C	Y	A	T	A	C	C	Y
M	T	A	P	R	X	M	T	A	P	R	X	M	T	A	P	R
I	M	R	I	N	H	I	M	R	I	N	H	I	M	R	I	N

© HarperCollins*Publishers* 2009

Worksheet: Bricklaying patterns

Wordsearch

D	E	S	P	G	O
L	T	A	O	C	O
A	T	S	R	N	L
A	T	A	C	C	Y
X	M	T	A	P	R
H	I	M	R	I	N

Task 2

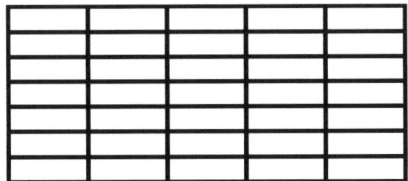 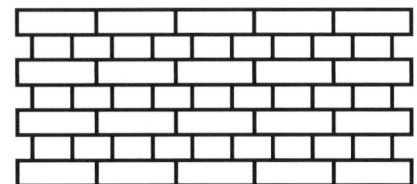

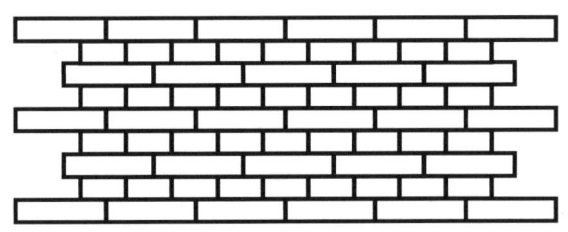 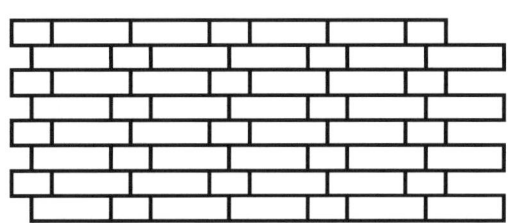

Task 3

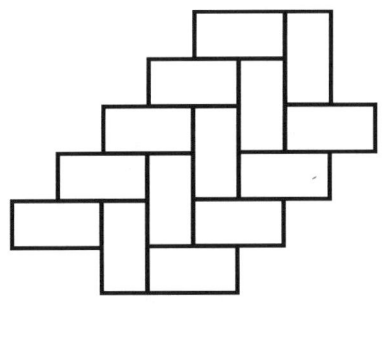 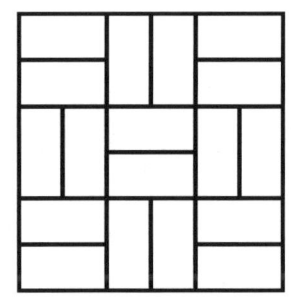

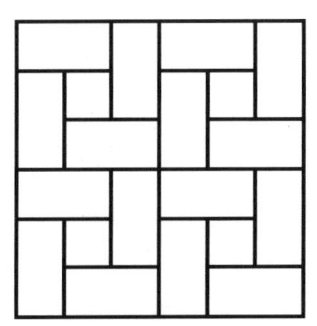 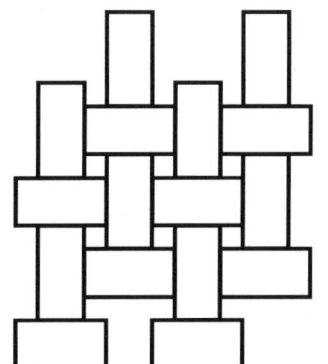

© HarperCollins*Publishers* 2009

Deliveries

Context

- The main tasks of this activity will be choosing routes to take and comparing distances.
- The teacher's role is to instruct the students to act as the manager of the warehouse and, in this role, to keep costs to a minimum by working out shortest routes and different strategies for carrying out the deliveries.
- The problem will develop into deciding whether to use extra vehicles, working out mileage costs and looking at practical advantages of using more than one vehicle.

Lesson plan

Starter

- Ask students to look at the first plan in the Pupil Book.
- Discuss different routes that could be taken, for example, W-A-B-C-W or W-B-C-A-W.
- Ask students to work through the warm-up questions. This could be done as a paired activity.

Main activity

- Ask students to look at Task 1 and ask: 'How many different routes can you work out?' Remind them that they have to start and finish at the warehouse.
- Ask students to complete Task 1.
- Now ask them to look at Task 2. Explain that the problem is the same as that in Task 1 but that now there are obviously more routes to consider.
- Again, remind students that they have to start and finish at the warehouse.
- Discuss strategies with the students. They could list all the routes systematically, for example, ABCD, ABDC, ACBD and so on, or use trial and improvement. There are $4 \times 3 \times 2 \times 1 = 24$ different routes without revisiting a depot.
- Explain that a company would plan routes carefully to save money. Explain also that whatever method they use they will need to keep a record of the results.
- Ask students to complete Task 2.
- Explain that in Task 3 the company is expanding and is therefore deciding whether to use two delivery vans. One of the vans could simply go to one depot and return while the other van goes to three depots, or they could go to two depots each. The task is to work out the shortest possible distances, using two vans.
- Now introduce the other variables. Point out that the vans cost 80p per mile to run. Ask them to work out how much more it costs to use two vans than one van.

Learning objectives

Representing: decide how to show the initial problem, using mathematical symbols; decide which methods to use to make progress with the solution

Analysing: analyse a pattern or a relationship using appropriate techniques

Interpreting: interpret results and solutions and make a generalisation about them; check that a conclusion is appropriate and accurate in the context of the original problem

Performing: use a range of mathematics to find solutions

APP: evidence for Using and applying mathematics, Calculating

PLTS: develops Creative thinkers, Team workers

Underpinning maths:
measures
money
time
extracting information from tables, diagrams and charts
collecting and recording data
organising and representing information in different ways

© HarperCollins*Publishers* 2009

Beginner

Resources
Pupil Book page 26
internet access
Worksheet: Deliveries

- Discuss advantages and disadvantages of using two vans; for example, advantage: deliveries would be quicker but disadvantage: it would be more expensive.
- For students to complete Task 4, either invite them to use the internet to find the mileages required or use the following chart (available on Worksheet: Deliveries).

	Huddersfield	Leeds	Nottingham	Sheffield	York
Huddersfield		20	54	30	45
Leeds	20		70	35	25
Nottingham	54	70		42	80
Sheffield	30	35	42		55
York	45	25	80	55	

Plenary

- Compare the results from different groups for each task.
- Ask groups who have the best answers to explain how they found them.

Extension work (open-ended)

- Ask students to think what other variables a manager might need to consider, for example, drivers' wages, time taken, number of parcels for each depot, size of vans.
- Students will need to realise that larger vans will cost more to run.
- They may want to look at vehicle rental costs and base their costing more realistically on these.
- Encourage students to cost their own models.
- Students could then extend Task 4 to include more towns and cities.
- Students could use internet searches to extend the task further.

Outcomes

- Students will have had opportunities to use mathematics to investigate practical problems.
- Students will have had practice in applying mathematics in an unfamiliar context.

© HarperCollins*Publishers* 2009

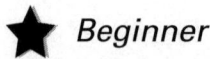
Beginner

Answers

Warm-up questions

1. 23 miles
2. 22 minutes
3. 6 journeys
4. 150 × 80p = £120
5. 6 × £120 = £720

Task 1

32 miles

Task 2

46 miles

Task 3

10 + 12 + 8 = 30 miles and 6 + 11 + 12 = 29 miles

Therefore it is more expensive to use two vans but deliveries are quicker.

Task 4

With one van it is 217 miles from Sheffield to Huddersfield to Leeds to York to Nottingham to Sheffield.

With two vans there are various answers. It would be best to send one to Nottingham and the other to Huddersfield, Leeds and York.

Beginner

Worksheet: Deliveries

	Huddersfield	Leeds	Nottingham	Sheffield	York
Huddersfield		20	54	30	45
Leeds	20		70	35	25
Nottingham	54	70		42	80
Sheffield	30	35	42		55
York	45	25	80	55	

Water

Context
- Water is vital to life and something that everyone tends to take for granted.
- Most households get water from the **mains system** and have waste water and sewage taken away via the pubic **sewerage system**.
- The cost of this service varies among different water companies but the basic principles apply to the way that any water bill is calculated.

Lesson plan

Starter
- Ask students if they can describe the capacity described as one litre. A good guide is that a typical can of soft drink is one-third of a litre, so three cans make up a litre, most small bottles of water contain half a litre. Larger bottles of water may contain two litres.
- If possible have a variety of everyday containers, such as three drinks cans or a two-litre water bottle, available to give a visual demonstration of the quantity in a way to which students will be able to relate.
- Ask students how they use water in any one day. They will soon establish washing, flushing toilets, cooking, washing up, washing clothes, watering plants, etc.
- Ask students how much water they think they use in a day. Answers are likely to be very low. In fact the figure is 150 litres. Looking at the containers gives a dramatic demonstration of just how much this is.

Main activity
- Look at the typical household bill in the Pupil Book.
- Explain each part of the bill.
- Make sure students understand that the standing charges are the same for all households and represent a **basic charge**.
- The other two parts of the bill depend on the rateable value of the property, in this case £240. This figure is multiplied by the rate for the supply of water and removing waste and sewage per pound of rateable value.
- Ask students why every property has a rateable value. They should suggest that it is to differentiate between large and small houses and to reflect the likely usage of water.
- It may be a worthwhile diversion to discuss if this system is fair. They could carry out an internet search to find out how rateable values compare in different areas.
- Make sure students understand how the bill is calculated.
- Now ask them to look at the pie chart of water use. This gives the average percentage of water that is used each day. Watering the garden or washing the car will not necessarily be a daily activity so the figures are averaged out.

Learning objectives

Representing: decide how to represent the problem to make it easier to solve using mathematics

Analysing: establish a pattern or relationship and then change the variables to see how this changes the results

Interpreting: give a conclusion or answer to the original problem, using language and forms of presentation that make sense to a wider population

Performing: use mathematical skills and knowledge to make progress on a real-life problem, even if the situation described is not within a familiar context; draw a conclusion from working and provide a mathematical justification for this conclusion

APP: evidence for Handling data, Shape, space and measures, Calculating

PLTS: develops Team workers, Effective participators

Cross-curricular links: ICT, Art

Beginner

- Students may need to be reminded how to calculate percentages. For example, 8% of 250 is 0.08 × 250 = 20; 13% of 330 is 0.13 × 330 = 42.9.
- Students can now do the tasks.

Plenary

- Discuss with students ways of conserving water.
- Keep the discussion sensible, not washing may appeal to many students!
- Discuss the effects that climate change seems to be having on the water cycle.
- There are many excellent diagrams available on the internet that show the water cycle. Students could carry out internet searches.
- Many countries experience droughts which mean that crops cannot grow
- Other countries have floods that destroy homes and crops.

Extension work

- There are many websites on saving water, including one from the UK government. Students could carry out an internet search, then produce a poster or a slide presentation.
  Simple tips are:
  - Don't run the tap when cleaning teeth.
  - Fit a water displacement device in the cistern (or use a brick).
  - When replacing appliances, buy water efficient machines.
  - Fit a water butt to collect rainwater from gutters.

Outcomes

- Students will have used basic mathematics to get insight into a everyday topic that affects us at the local and global level.

Underpinning maths:
basic numeracy
estimation
reading pie charts
percentages
metric units

Resources
Pupil Book page 29
computers
internet access

© HarperCollins*Publishers* 2009

 *Beginner*

Answers

Task 1

1   Toilets: 38 litres; baths: 50 litres; drinking/cooking: 20 litres; dishwashing: 12 litres; clothes: 21 litres; other: 11 litres

2   4.55

Task 2

Volume of a brick = 1432 cm³ = 1.432 litres, 6 flushes × 365 = 2190 flushes; saving over a year: 2190 × 1.432 = 3136 ≈ 3140 litres

Task 3

1   £35.80 + 200 × 1.075 + 39.78 + 1.68 + 200 × 1.227 = £537.66

2   £35.80 + 175 × 1.075 + 39.78 + 1.68 + 175 × 1.227 = £480.11

3   £35.80 + 240 × 0.993 + 39.78 + 1.68 + 240 × 1.154 = £592.54; saving £37.20

Task 4

1   £35.80 + 39.78 + 1.68 + 3 × 150 × 365 × 0.003 = £570.01; saving £59.73

2   200 ÷ 59.73 = 3.34, so approximately 3 years 4 months

Task 5

1   77.5 litres

2   4 × 365 × 140 = 204 400 litres; this is 204 400 ÷ 77.5 = 2637 bathtubs

© HarperCollins*Publishers* 2009

Safe flying over the UK

Context
- The activity is about reading information from tables and charts and accessing key data.
- It is also about interpreting the information and presenting it in a variety of forms.

Lesson plan

Starter
- Ensure that students understand eight-point compass bearings and can identify each of the eight directions.
- Test their knowledge by asking the students to label an eight-point compass diagram.
- Ask the students how high they think jets fly. Answers will usually be given by someone who has travelled by air when going on holiday. Common responses are 30 000 feet or 40 000 feet.
- Point out that 1000 feet is about one-fifth of a mile.
(5280 feet = 1 mile)

Main activity
- The main activity involves three-figure bearings.
- Start by drawing some three-figure bearings to demonstrate the direction that an aircraft would be flying when on a bearing of, for example, 045° (north-east), 090° (east), 135° (south-east), 180° (due south), 225° (south-west), 270° (west), 315° (north-west) and 000° (due north).
- Ask the students to read the information given about flight levels.
- State a flight level and ask students to give the corresponding altitude, in feet. Repeat for several different flight levels.
- State an altitude, in feet, and ask students to give the corresponding flight level. Repeat for several different altitudes.
- Now ask students to look at the semi-circular rule.
- Give out directions as three-figure bearings and ask students to give a possible flight level. Repeat for eight-point compass bearings. Then give three-figure and eight-point compass bearings randomly.
- Now ask students to work through the questions.

Plenary
- Ask students what they have learned.
- Summarise the information given.
- Use a compass to determine the direction of north. Ask students to imagine an aircraft was flying over the classroom in a particular direction and to estimate the three-figure bearing of the direction of flight of this aircraft.

Learning objectives

Representing: recognise that a real-life problem can be solved using appropriate mathematics

Analysing: analyse a pattern or a relationship using appropriate techniques

Interpreting: give a conclusion or answer to the original problem, using language and forms of presentation that make sense to a wider population

Performing: give a solution to a practical problem, even if it is not within a familiar context, and make sure the solution is presented in a clear and understandable way; draw a conclusion from working and provide a mathematical justification for this conclusion

APP: evidence for Using and applying mathematics, Shape, space and measures

PLTS: develops Effective participators, Creative thinkers

Cross-curricular links: ICT

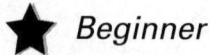 *Beginner*

Extension work

- Ask students to search the internet to find out about the **quadrantal rule**.
- Alternatively, explain the rule (given below) and ask students to complete a diagram to represent the information, similar to the diagram given for the **semi-circular rule**.

Underpinning maths:
eight-point compass directions
three-figure bearings
multiplication and division by powers of 10

The quadrantal rule for aircraft flying outside controlled airspace above 300 feet
- Magnetic track 000–089° – odd thousands of feet (FL 70, 90, 110 etc.)
- Magnetic track 090–179° – odd thousands + 500 feet (FL 75, 95, 115 etc.)
- Magnetic track 180–269° – even thousands of feet (FL 80, 100, 120 etc.)
- Magnetic track 270–359° – even thousands + 500 feet (FL 85, 105, 125 etc.)

Outcomes

- Students will have had opportunities to tackle practical problems in unfamiliar contexts, identifying and obtaining necessary information.
- Students will have selected and applied mathematics in an organised way.
- Students will have interpreted and communicated solutions, giving explanations.

Resources
Pupil Book page 32
compass
internet access

Answers

1. FL 65
2. 28 000 feet
3. Flight levels go up in fives (500 feet at a time) so FL30 is followed by FL35.
4. FL 110 or FL 130
5. FL 100 or FL 120
6. FL 100 or FL 120
7. FL 110 or FL 130
8. 1000 feet
9. 2000 feet
10. 4000 feet

© HarperCollins*Publishers* 2009

Darts

Context
- This activity requires skills with basic numeracy and breaking problems down, within the medium of the well-known game of darts.
- Darts emerged as a popular game in English public houses early in the 20th century but it had been around in various forms for much longer than that.
- It is thought that the game originated when archers amused themselves by throwing their arrows at the ends of barrels.

Lesson plan
Starter
- Provide a target board with the numbers 1 to 20 and ask students to double or treble the scores. This would give practice in some of the basic numeracy skills required for this task.
- Alternatively, or as well, discuss the game of darts. Most students will have some idea of the game and the basic principles. If not go through the introductory text in the Pupil Book.
- The main points about the dartboard are the **triple** and **double** scores, the **inner bull** and the **outer bull**.
- There are many different darts games but the one used in professional darts is **501**. Players have to score 501 as soon as possible and finish on a double (reducing their score from 501 to zero). Make sure students understand that a double has to be scored to finish the game.

> There are many free darts games available on the internet. A search on 'Free to play darts games' will bring up several results, including one for Smilie.
> Most interactive whiteboards also have a darts package, which can be used to find three-dart finishes for various numbers.

- Challenge a student to play an online game with you or get two students to play each other.
- When the game is approaching a **finish**, encourage discussion as to the best option.

Main activity
- Once students have gained the basic ideas of scoring, doubles, trebles and finishing on a double ask a series of questions.
  - What is the greatest score possible? How is it obtained? (180, T20)
  - Can you score every value less than 180? (No: six scores are not possible with three darts, 179, 178, 176, 175, 173 and 172)

Learning objectives
Analysing: find a result or solution to the original problem

Interpreting: interpret results and solutions and make a generalisation about them

Performing: analyse a situation or problem and decide which is the appropriate mathematical method needed to tackle it

APP: evidence for Calculating

PLTS: develops Independent enquirers, Team workers

Underpinning maths:
multiplication by 2 and by 3
addition of three numbers, each up to 60

Resources
Pupil Book page 35
target board with the numbers 1 to 20
internet access

© HarperCollins*Publishers* 2009

★ *Beginner*

- What is the highest score it is possible to finish on? (170: T20, T20, D20)
- Is there a finish for all scores below 170? (No, 169, 168, 166, 165, 163, 162 and 159 do not have three-dart finishes)
- What would a finish be for 160? (T20, T20, D20)
- Is this the only finish for 160? (No: T20, bull, bull also possible)
- What is the lowest three-dart finish? (4: S1, S1, D1)
- What is the highest two-dart finish? (110: T20, bull)

- Students can then work together in small groups to do the exercise.
- Note that Question 1 is designed to give some basic practice and introduce them to the notation, T for treble, D for double and S for single.
- The extension question can be used as enrichment or set for homework.

Plenary

- Discuss strategies for mental calculation of doubles and trebles, for example:
  $3 \times 18 = 3 \times 10 + 3 \times 8 = 30 + 24 = 54$
- Move on to multiplying by 4 (double and double) and possibly halving, dividing by 4, for example:
  $14 \div 4 \Rightarrow 14 \div 2 = 7, 7 \div 2 = 3.5$

Outcomes

- Students will have practised some basic numeracy skills.
- Students will have used some basic problem-solving skills in breaking numbers down to find different combinations of doubles and trebles.
- Students will have worked cooperatively with others.

Answers

1. **a** 69 **b** 91 **c** 54 **d** 77 **e** 83

2. **a** Any finish that gives a total of 60 for the first two darts, e.g. D20, S20

   b Any finish that gives a total of 50 for the first two darts, e.g. D20, S10

   c Any finish that gives a total of 68 for the first two darts, e.g. T20, S8

3. **a** 180 **b** 23

4. **a** e.g. T19, D9 **b** S60, D19 **c** S1, D1

5. The largest number that can be scored with one dart is 60, so 99 − 60 = 39. 39 cannot be scored with 1 dart.

6. 23, 29, 31, 35, 37, 41, 43, 44, 46, 47, 49, 52, 53, 55, 56, 58, 59

7. **a** 10 and 14; 9 and 15 **b** 18 + 7 = 25 **c** 12 + 2 = 14

8. **a** 16 and 4; 5 and 17 **b** 14 − 10 = 4 **c** 19 − 1 = 18

9. **a** 10 and 15, 11 and 14 **b** 6 + 10 = 16

   c 1 + 18, 13 + 6, 2 + 17, 8 + 11 **d** 19 + 7 = 26

© HarperCollins*Publishers* 2009

Beginner

10   Adding pairs of numbers 10 + 11, 9 + 12, 8 + 13, 7 + 14, 6 + 15, etc. all give a total of 21.

There are 10 lots of these, so 10 × 21 = 210

Extension question

First three darts: 3 × T20 = 180, leaving 501 − 180 = 321; second three darts: 3 × T20 = 180, leaving 321 − 180 = 141; 141 has several three-dart finishes, e.g. T20, T19, D12 or T19, T18, D15

Bridges

Context
- This activity is about reading information from tables and charts and accessing key data.
- It is also about interpreting information and presenting it in a variety of forms.
- It culminates in the very open-ended task of designing a bridge, which is best done by students working in small groups.

Lesson plan

Starter
- Ensure that students know the technical words related to bridges, for example, **suspension bridge**, **span**, **supports**.
- Ask the students how long they think the longest suspension bridge in the world is, and where it is.
- Give the students the Data sheet: Bridges and let them read through it.
- Ask students to write half a million in figures (500 000), using their mini-whiteboards.
- Ask students to look at the table of the eight longest single-span suspension bridges and put them in order of age, from oldest to newest.

Main activity
- Use Tasks 1 and 2 to test whether the students can derive information from other information that is given.
- These tasks can be extended by asking students to use internet searches to find information about other bridges and comparing facts; for example, the amount of steel used or the span of the bridges.
- Students could also research the new suspension bridge, planned to stretch for more than two miles across the Strait of Messina, from Sicily to the region of Calabria in Italy. If built, it will be the longest yet.
- Task 3 may be the most challenging and will need to be discussed before starting.
- Students will need to work in small groups and will need a collection of resources as suggested. The aim is not just to build a bridge according to the instructions but to try to design a bridge that also looks good. Judging the results to decide the best bridge may not be easy.

Plenary
- Ask students to tell you about the best features of their constructions.
- Ask students to test the strength of their bridges with objects that are heavier than calculators.

Learning objectives

Representing: decide which methods to use to make progress with the solution

Analysing: use appropriate mathematical procedures

Interpreting: test generalisations and draw conclusions from the mathematical analysis

Performing: analyse the situation or problem and decide which is the appropriate mathematical method needed to tackle it; give a solution to a practical problem, even if it is not within a familiar context, and make sure the solution is presented in a clear and understandable way

APP: evidence for Using and applying mathematics, Shape, space and measures

PLTS: develops Team workers, Creative thinkers

Cross-curricular links: ICT, Geography, Science, Design and Technology

Underpinning maths: basic number work

© HarperCollins*Publishers* 2009

Improver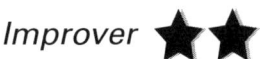

Extension work
- Students could try to make a bridge with a wider span or combine the designs from several groups.

Outcomes
- Students will have used mathematics to gain insight into a real-life problem.
- Students will have extracted information from tables.
- Students will have worked cooperatively with others.

Resources
Pupil Book page 38
mini-whiteboards
drinking straws
sheets of A4 paper
rubber bands
paper clips
sticky tape
internet access
Data sheet: Bridges

Answers
Task 1

1   9 years

2   About 6 million

3   480 000 tonnes

4   Akashi Kaikyo and Jiangyin Jiangsu (30 metres)

5   80 kilometres

6   17 years

7   130 metres

8   £1.50

9   £15 396 866.10

10 25%

Task 2

Golden Gate – Over 50 years old

© HarperCollins*Publishers* 2009

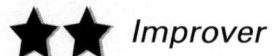 *Improver*

Data sheet: Bridges

Work started on building the Humber Bridge in **1972**.

The Humber Bridge was **opened by the Queen** in **July 1981**.

Before the bridge was built people used to cross the Humber by **ferry**. This usually took about **20 minutes**.

Ths distance from **Hull to Grimsby**, using the motorway around the Humber, is about **50 miles further** than using the bridge.

The bridge carries about **half a million vehicles per month**.

480 000 tonnes of concrete were used to build the bridge.

The **main span** of the bridge is **1410 metres**.

The **total length between anchorages is 2220 metres**.

The **main cables** are made from **11 000 tonnes of steel wire**, which is enough to stretch **43 000 miles** or **one and a half times around the Earth**.

The life-span of the bridge is **120 years**.

Ticket prices

Motor cycle: £1.20
Car: £2.70
Heavy goods vehicles (HGV): up to £18.30

Record-breaking single-span suspension bridges

Name	Country	Span (metres)	Year of opening to traffic	Carriageway width (metres)
Akashi Kaikyo	Japan	1990	1998	30.0
Great Belt	Denmark	1624	1998	23.6
Runyang	China	1490	2005	39.2
Humber	England	1410	1981	18.2
Jiangyin Jiangsu	China	1385	1999	30.0
Tsing Ma	Hong Kong	1377	1997	30.7
Verrazano Narrows	USA	1298	1964	25.3
Golden Gate	USA	1280	1937	25.0

Money matters 2: Tax and national insurance

Context
- This is the second of five activities that deal with the money issues that students will meet during their lifetimes.
- The mathematics involved is basic numeracy and students are recommended to use calculators.

Lesson plan

Starter
- It would be useful to review percentages and ensure that students can identify the percentage multiplier. Percentages that need to be calculated include 20%, 40%, 11% and 1%.
- Students should understand that 20% of £264 can be calculated easily as 0.2 × 264 (= 52.8).

Main activity
- Students have already met the basic ideas of workers being paid in the form of wages or a salary. They have already discussed the typical deductions that are taken off the gross earnings.
- Review the concept of gross earnings and deductions. Ask students what tax is used to pay for.
- Students will probably know about tax but may be less familiar with national insurance (NI). Explain that national insurance is used essentially to fund the benefits system, which includes the state pension, sickness pay and unemployment benefit.
- Explain that everyone has a tax allowance, which is the amount a worker is allowed to earn before any income tax is due. The rate in 2009–10 is £6475. Students can use an internet search to find the current allowance.
- After the tax allowance is deducted from earnings the rest is the taxable income. Of this the first £37 400 (at 2009–10 rates) is taxed at 20% and the rest is taxed at 40%. Students can use an internet search to find the current rates.
- Make sure students understand the PAYE system, under which tax is deducted each time a worker is paid. This means that there is no large tax bill at the end of the year and the Government has a regular source of money.
- Explain the NI system. This is quite complicated so it has been simplified for the purposes of this activity. The first £110 earned each week is not counted for NI contributions. Any weekly earnings above this up, to £844, are assessed at 11%. Any earnings above £844 are assessed at 1%. These are 2009–10 rates. Students can use an internet search to find the current rates.

Learning objectives

Representing: decide how to represent the problem to make it easier to solve using mathematics

Analysing: find a result or solution to the original problem

Performing: use mathematical skills and knowledge to make progress on a real-life problem, even if the situation described is not within a familiar context

APP: evidence for Calculating

PLTS: develops Independent enquirers

Cross-curricular links: ICT

Underpinning maths:
basic numeracy
percentages

Resources
Pupil Book page 40
internet access

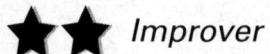 *Improver*

- Work through the two examples in the Pupil Book with the students.
- Ask students to answer the questions in the Pupil Book.

Plenary

- Discuss the concepts and mathematics the students have used.
- Explain that many workers have to submit a self-assessment form each year, detailing earnings and tax paid.
- For most people this is based on a P60, which is a form that employers give employees at the end of each tax year.
- However, there are other factors that need to be considered. Interest on savings accounts and dividends from stocks and shares have to be declared.
- Eventually, Her Majesty's Revenue and Customs (HMRC) either gives a tax rebate or asks for a further contribution. If this is under £2000 it is usually collected by adjusting the personal allowance for the following year.

Extension work

- Students could search on the internet to find out how the Government spends its tax income. They could find out what proportion goes on the National Health Service, for example.

Outcomes

- Students will have had the opportunity to use basic numeracy in a real-life situation.

Answers

1. Annual income: £11 440; taxable income: £4965; 20% of 4965 = £993; weekly tax: £19.10; NI: 11% of £110 = £12.10; total deductions: £31.20; weekly take-home pay: £188.80

2. Taxable income: £37 525.; tax paid: 20% of £37 400 + 40% of £125 = £7530; monthly tax: £627.50; weekly pay: £846.15; NI: 11% of £734 + 1% of £2.15 = £80.76; monthly NI: £80.76 × 52 ÷ 12 = £349.96; monthly net salary: £3666.67 − (£349.96 + £627.50) = £2689.21

3. Annual salary: £30 000; taxable income: £23 525; 20% of 23 525 = £4705; monthly tax: £392.08; weekly income: £30 000 ÷ 52 = £576.92; NI: 11% of £466.92 = £51.36; monthly NI: £222.56; monthly net salary: £2500 − £392.08 − £222.56 = £1885.36

4. Annual income: £28 600; taxable income: £22 125; 20% of £22 125 = £4425; weekly tax: £4425 ÷ 52 = £85.10; NI: 11% of £440 = £48.40; net weekly wage: £550 − £85.10 − £48.40 = £416.50

5. Mr T: annual income: £19 760; taxable income: £13 285; 20% of £13 285 = £2657; weekly tax: £51.10; NI: 11% of £270 = £29.70; Mrs T: annual income: £6760; taxable income: £285; 20% of 285 = 57; weekly tax: £1.10; NI: 11% of 20 = £2.20; total income: £510; total weekly deductions: (£51.10 + £29.70 + £1.10 + £2.20; net weekly income: £425.90

Improver ★★

6 Mr U: taxable income: £45 525; tax: 20% of £37 400 + 40% of £8125 = £10 730; monthly tax: £894.17; weekly income: £1000; N1: 11% of £734 + 1% of £156 = £82.30; monthly NI: £356.63; Ms V: taxable income: £51 525. Tax: 20% of £37 400 + 40% of £14 125 = £13 130; monthly tax: £1094.17; weekly income: £1115.38; N1: 11% of £734 + 1% of £271.38 = £83.45; monthly NI: £361.62; monthly joint income: £9166.67; monthly deductions: £894.17 + £356.63 + £1094.17 + £361.62; net monthly joint income: £6460.08

7 Before pay rise: annual income: £36 000; taxable income: £29 525; 20% of £29 525 = £5905; monthly tax: £492.08; weekly pay: £692.31; 11% of £582.31 = £64.05; monthly NI: £277.57; take-home monthly before rise: £2230.35. After pay rise: annual income: 6 × £3000 + 6 × £3500 = £39 000; taxable income: £32 525; 20% of £32 525 = £6505; monthly tax: £542.08; weekly pay: £807.69; 11% of £697.69 = £76.75; monthly NI: £332.57; take-home monthly pay after rise: £2625.35; increase: £395.

8 **a** taxable income = £17 525, tax = 20% of £17 525 = £3505

   b Taxable income = £9525, tax = 20% of £9525 = £1905

   c £1600

Extension work

The NHS used about 9% of Gross Domestic Product (total government income) in 2008 but tends to increase each year.

Revision planning

Context
- This activity is about planning carefully and following rules.
- It involves making the best use of time.

Lesson plan

Starter
- Ask students to write down five revision tips that they find useful.
- Collate a list on the board.
- Keep a tally of those tips that are repeated so that you can compile the 'Top ten tips'.

Main activity
- Explain that the activity is about planning revision effectively.
- Point out that a revision timetable is of little use if the student cannot stick to it.
- Explain that the activity is about a Year 11 student who takes 11 subjects. To shorten the task, the number of subjects could be reduced. Tables are also provided on Worksheet: Revision planning if required.
- Look at the conditions for Task 1. These can be adapted to suit the ability of the group.
- It is important to stress that there will be spaces in the revision planning table when it is complete and that these spaces could be used to reduce the daily commitment or to have a day off.
- Ask students to plan the revision as they would like to do it.
- Students can now complete Task 1.
- Task 2 introduces more variables into the plan and allows students to make more of their own decisions.
- Look at the changes to the conditions with the students before they start the task.
- Task 3 invites the students to plan a revision programme for their own subjects and circumstances. It might be helpful to discuss and agree with the students some conditions before they start this task.

Plenary
- Ask students to show each other their revision plans to check and discuss them.
- Ask them to compare their plans and identify the best features.

Extension work
- Ask students to design a poster based on the 'Top ten tips' for revision.

Outcomes
- Students will have analysed a situation and reach a conclusion.
- Students will have made sure the solution is presented in a clear and understandable way.
- Students will have used some simple mathematics to gain insight into a relevant situation.

Learning objectives

Representing: recognise that a real-life problem can be solved using appropriate mathematics; decide which methods to use to make progress with the solution; decide how to represent the problem to make it easier to solve using mathematics

Analysing: analyse a pattern or a relationship using appropriate techniques; find a result or solution to the original problem

Interpreting: interpret results and solutions and make a generalisation about them

Performing: use a range of mathematics to find solutions

APP: evidence for Using and applying mathematics, Calculating

PLTS: develops Independent enquirers, Creative thinkers

Cross-curricular links: ICT, Design and Technology

Underpinning maths:
time
reasoning
planning

Resources
Pupil Book page 43
Worksheet: Revision planning

© HarperCollins Publishers 2009

Improver

Worksheet: Revision planning

Task 1

	6.00 pm–6.30 pm	6.30 pm–7.00 pm	7.00 pm–7.15 pm	7.15 pm–7.45 pm	7.45 pm–8.15 pm	8.15 pm–8.30 pm	8.30 pm–9.00 pm	9.00 pm–9.30 pm
Monday			Break			Break		
Tuesday								
Wednesday								
Thursday								
Friday								
Saturday								
Sunday								

Task 2

	6.00 pm–6.30 pm	6.30 pm–7.00 pm	7.00 pm–7.15 pm	7.15 pm–7.45 pm	7.45 pm–8.15 pm	8.15 pm–8.30 pm	8.30 pm–9.00 pm	9.00 pm–9.30 pm
Monday			Break			Break		
Tuesday								
Wednesday								
Thursday								
Friday								

	10.00 am–						
Saturday							
Sunday							

© HarperCollins*Publishers* 2009

At the gym

Context
- This unusual context is unlikely to be familiar to students. This activity is about distributions and using them to make estimates.

Lesson plan

Starter
- Before looking in the Pupil Book it may be useful to look at a copy of the plan of the showers.
- Discuss with the students how the showers are likely to be used. For example:
  - 'Would any of the showers get used more than any other? Why?'
  - 'If there were soap dispensers, would they get used at an equal rate? Why?'
- The drawing is to scale with each square representing half a metre.
- Some work on scales and area could be done.
- Also ask students how they would expect the gym to be used during the day?
  - 'When would it be busiest?'
  - 'Would the use by men and women follow a similar pattern?'
- This will set up the tasks in students' minds.

Main activity
- Ask students to read the introductory text in the Pupil Book.
- Ensure they understand the context and the distributions.
- Ask questions about the soap dispensers such as:
  - 'How much do the containers hold altogether when full?' (2500 ml)
  - 'What is this in litres? (2.5 litres)
  - 'How much soap is left in shower 3?' (350 ml)
  - 'How much soap was used in shower 2?' (300 ml)
  - 'How much soap was used altogether?' (1 litre)
- In Task 1 and Task 2, students are asked to interpret the distributions of the soap used and the numbers of men entering the gym during the day.
- The answers to these could be discussed as a class.
- Interpretation of distributions in real-life situations is important and students should be encouraged to provide a sensible and complete description.
- For example, in response to a question about the use of showers, just saying: 'More people use shower 1,' would be correct but would not be a complete answer.
- Ask them to describe the use of soap if the entrance to the showers was in the centre, for example, opposite the middle cubicle.
- Ask questions about the distribution of men entering the gym:
  - 'When was the busiest time?' (5 pm–7 pm)
  - 'How many men entered between 7 am and 8 am?' (22)
  - 'How many men entered between 11 am and 2 pm?' (74)

Learning objectives

Representing: recognise that a real-life problem can be solved using appropriate mathematics

Interpreting: interpret results and solutions and make a generalisation about them; check that a conclusion is appropriate and accurate in the context of the original problem

Performing: use mathematical skills and knowledge to make progress on a real-life problem, even if the situation described is not a familiar context; draw a conclusion from working and provide a mathematical justification for this conclusion

APP: evidence for Using and applying mathematics, Handling data

PLTS: develops Creative thinkers, Effective participators

Underpinning maths:
reading scales
reading graphs
estimation
metric units

Resources
Pupil Book page 46
Worksheet: At the gym

Improver ★★

- Ask them if the distribution would be any different if the gym opened from 5 am to 11 pm (likely to be very few people before 6 or after 9) or if it was open 24 hours, as some gyms in large cities are (likely to have a few people through the night).
- Ask students to complete Task 3, to find the total soap used in the showers on the Monday in question. They will need to find the use of soap per person up to 9 am and extrapolate this for the whole day.
- Ask them to describe the likely distribution for Saturday and Sunday (likely to be fairly consistent through the day). This is Task 4.
- Make sure students do not misinterpret the scales.
- Task 5 builds on the work in the previous tasks and looks at a possible solution to the need to check soap dispensers so often.

Plenary

- Discuss with students what they have learned from doing this task.
- Ask them what differences there may have been had the distributions been produced for women who belong to the gym. Would they show a similar situation?
- The soap distribution may well be similar, in that shower 1 would still be used more often. In reality women may use more soap, or they may use less if they take their own cleaning products into the shower. The pattern of women visiting the gym may be different, as those who do not go out to work may come during mid-morning and mid-afternoon, although professional women may follow a similar pattern to men.

Outcomes

- Students will have used mathematics to model a real-life situation.
- Students will have extracted information from graphs.
- Students will have interpreted distributions.

Answers

Task 1

Most people will use the nearest shower; as shower 1 is nearest the entrance this will be used first if it is available. That is why shower 1 has almost run out and shower 5 hasn't been used.

Task 2

Some men come in very early and then a few more arrive before work. It then gets quieter until lunchtime when more men arrive; it goes quiet during the afternoon and peaks after work.

Task 3

Between 6 am and 9 am, 60 men visit the gym. In that time 1 litre of soap is used. This is $1000 \div 60 = 16.67$ ml per person on average.

During the day 320 men visit the gym. This is $320 \times 16.67 = 5334.4$ ml of soap ≈ 5.3 litres.

© HarperCollins*Publishers* 2009

Task 4

The bar chart should run from 9 am to 5 pm, with most bars about 20 ml units high but with the bars around 12 midday to 2 pm slightly higher.

Task 5

   a   Approximately 1.1 litres

   b   On the previous Monday, in shower 1, 450 ml of soap had been used by 9 am. This Monday 300 ml has been used.

This is about 100 ml per hour, so the soap in shower 1 should last 5 hours. The latest time to get them checked is 11 am.

Task 6 (extension)

Any sensible program, for example:

15 minutes kick boxing (150 calories), 10 minutes light weights (70 calories), 10 minutes light rowing (70 calories), 10 minutes jogging on treadmill (100 calories), 15 minutes aerobics (105 calories). Total 1 hour and 495 calories.

Tour de France: 5900 calories per day on average.

Marathon: 2600 calories during a marathon.

Football match: 1000 calories for a professional player.

Worksheet: At the gym

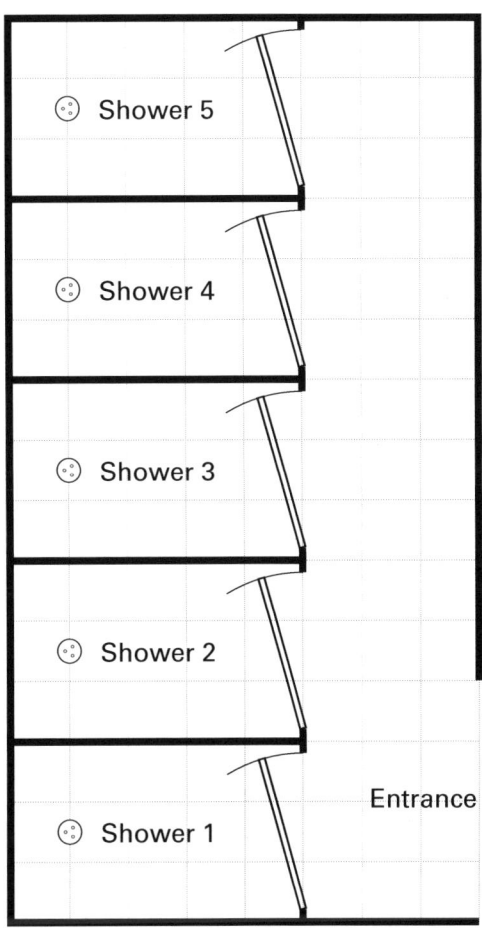

Money matters 3: Loans and APR

Context
- The lesson is about interpreting information given in unfamiliar forms.
- It is a **pre-requisite** that students know how to work out a **percentage of a quantity**.

Lesson plan

Starter
- Start with a mental test on simple percentages, for example:
    - What is 1% of £100?
    - What is 5% of £100?
    - What is 7% of £100?
    - What is 7.8% of £100?
    - What is 7.8% of £1000?
    - How would you work out 7.8% of £5000?
- Students could use mini-whiteboards to give their answers.
- Explain about APR. Explain that it is a fair way of comparing interest rates on loans.
- Talk through the five advertisements with the students.
- Now ask students to answer the **warm-up questions**, giving the answers as you go along. The warm-up questions do not compare loans but simply make the students familiar with the way that loans operate.

Main activity
- The main activity involves **annual percentage rate (APR)** rather than calculation of actual amounts of interest, although students will need to do this in later work.
- Explain how some loans, usually short-term loans, often appear more attractive than they are and that the APR can be very high. (See The Instant Cash Loans Company.)
- Ask students to look at Task 1.
- Ask the students to sort the advertisements into order of 'best loan'. There is a worksheet for this task.
- Compare results to decide which is the best loan.
- See whether there is agreement between groups.
- Discuss the reasons why some loans seem cheaper than others, for example, when borrowing small amounts, the sum to repay does not seem very great.
- Carry out an internet search on **loan calculator**. Use the loan calculator to find out what the monthly repayments are on various amounts, APRs and different time periods. Results will appear something like this.

Learning objectives

Representing: recognise that a real-life problem can be solved using appropriate mathematics; decide how to show the initial problem using mathematical symbols

Analysing: establish a pattern or relationship and then change the variables to see how this changes the results

Interpreting: check that a conclusion is appropriate and accurate in the context of the original problem; give a conclusion or answer to the original problem, using language and forms of presentation that make sense to a wider population

Performing: use mathematical skills and knowledge to make progress on a problem, even if it does not use a routine mathematical procedure; use a range of mathematics to find solutions

APP: evidence for Using and applying mathematics, Calculating

PLTS: develops Independent enquirers, Self-managers

Cross-curricular links:
English, Art

Improver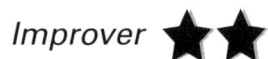

Enter loan details

Loan amount (£)	1000
Repayment period (years)	5
APR (%)	10
Number of payments per year	12

Calculate   Clear

Results

Amount per repayment (£)	21.25
Total paid over the life of the loan (£)	1274.82
Total interest paid during loan (£)	274.82

Underpinning maths:
percentage of a quantity
understanding of annual percentage rate (APR)

Resources
Pupil Book page 50
mini-whiteboards
internet access
Worksheet: Loans and APR

- When the students have completed Task 1, explain that some advertisements are easier to understand than others.
- Ask students to put the five advertisements in order of difficulty to understand, starting with the easiest. Discuss the meaning of words such as **consolidate**, **optional**, **debt**.
- Now ask students to look at Task 2. Explain that you want them to think up a good advertisement of their own, using the best parts of those shown in the Pupil Book.

Plenary

- Ask students to tell you what they liked about the advertisements and what they did not like.
- See if there is agreement between different groups.
- Let students present their advertisements and ask them to say why they are better than the ones given.

Outcomes

- Students will have had opportunities to understand practical problems in an unfamiliar context.
- Students will have identified necessary information and applied mathematics in an organised way.
- Students will have interpreted and communicated solutions, drawn simple conclusions and given explanations.

© HarperCollins*Publishers* 2009

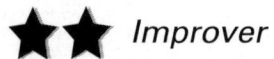 *Improver*

Answers

Warm-up questions

1 a £5000   b £25 000   c £78   d £390
2 a Monthly b £80 000   c £850   d £4250
3 a 1284%   b 25%   c Short-term loan
4 a Weekly   b £500   c Short-term loan with weekly repayments
5 a £20 000 b 5 years   c Repayment insurance

Task 1

Name of company	Online, branch or shop	Amount that can be borrowed	Repayments: one payment, weekly or monthly	APR
TopService Personal Loans	Online	£5000 to £25 000	Monthly	7.8%
Gordon's Cheap Loans	Branch or shop	£5000 to £100 000	Monthly	8.5%
The Instant Cash Loans Company	Telephone	Up to £1000	One payment	1284%
Cash Around the Corner Loans	Shop	£50 to £500	Weekly	189.2%
The Lending Bank	Online or branch	Up to £20 000	Monthly	9.9%

© HarperCollins*Publishers* 2009

Improver

Worksheet: Loans and APR
Task 1

Name of company	Online, branch or shop	Amount that can be borrowed	Repayments: one payment, weekly or monthly	APR
TopService Personal Loans	Online	£5000 to £25 000	Monthly	7.8%
Gordon's Cheap Loans				
The Instant Cash Loans Company				
Cash Around the Corner Loans				
The Lending Bank				

Stickers

Context
- Many students will be familiar with collecting Panini stickers.
- Despite the companies' claims that they print the same number of stickers in each set, there always seems to be a couple of stickers that never seem to turn up to compete a set.
- There are 3 tasks which use a mathematical model to replicate collecting a set of stickers given x stickers in the set which are sold in packs of y.

Lesson plan

Starter
- Ask students if any of them collect Panini or other brand stickers. Establish the basic principle that the company produces a set of stickers and an album in which to stick them.
- Ask students what the current sets represent. (At the time of publication, there were 17 sets on sale, two of which were the *Coca Cola Championship* and *High School Musical 3*.) Ask them how many there are in the sets in total. (At the time of publication, there are 384 in the *Coca Cola Championship* set and 186 in the *High School Musical 3* set.)
- Ask how many stickers there were in a pack. (At the time of publication, there are five in both the *Coca Cola Championship* and the *High School Musical 3* packs).
- Ask whether the packs ever contain duplicate cards. They should not but in the model below they might.
- Also ask how much a pack costs. (At the time of publication, the *Coca Cola Championship* packs cost 35p and the *High School Musical 3* packs cost 40p.)
- Ask students if, when they buy new packs, they always get new stickers they don't already have. As the packs are randomly put together this is unlikely, except for the first couple of packs.
- Discuss what they do with spares (swap, sell).
- Ask what they do when they have almost completed a set. Are the final few stickers they need easy to get or do some always seem to be elusive? They are likely to say that some stickers always seem hard to get and they may have to resort to internet sites to find the final few.

Main activity
- Explain that the class will use a mathematical model to replicate what happens when stickers are collected.
- Discuss Task 1. Ask students, in pairs or small groups, to make sets of five stickers. Stickers will be 'sold' in packs of three.
- It would be advisable to have at least one set of cards made beforehand, to demonstrate the process of modelling.

Learning objectives

Representing: decide which methods to use to make progress with the solution

Analysing: establish a pattern or relationship and then change the variables to see how this changes the results

Interpreting: interpret results and solutions and make a generalisation about them; test generalisations and draw conclusions from the mathematical analysis; check that a conclusion is appropriate and accurate in the context of the original problem

Performing: use mathematical skills and knowledge to make progress on a problem, even if it does not use a routine mathematical procedure; analyse the situation or problem and decide which is the appropriate mathematical method needed to tackle it; use a range of mathematics to find solutions

APP: evidence for Using and applying mathematics, Handling data

PLTS: develops Creative thinkers, Team workers

Cross-curricular links: ICT

© HarperCollins*Publishers* 2009

Improver ★★

Underpinning maths: experimental probability

- The prepared cards could show images of the Simpson family (Homer, Marge, Bart, Lisa and Maggie). This is suggested in the Pupil Book, where the students are invited to guess what H, M, B, L and Mg stand for. To save students time, cards could be pre-printed on A4 sheets.
- Model collecting a set of stickers, as outlined in the Pupil Book.
- Ask a student to record the outcomes on the board.
- Depending on the outcome of the trial ask questions such as:
  - What is the smallest number of packs needed to get a complete set? (two, as this would give six stickers which could possibly yield the five individual ones required)
  - What is the greatest number of packs that would be needed to complete a set? (in theory, an infinite number, as there is no guarantee that the last sticker will be in any pack)
  - Does it matter that once one sticker is obtained the chance of getting it again is reduced? (in theory, yes, as this is conditional probability but, as there are literally millions of stickers produced for any series, then in practice the answer is no)
- Now let students do Task 1. Note that it is important that they return the pack of three to the pool each time, as otherwise the random element is compromised.
- Once all the class have done Task 1 then results can be compared. Individual groups' results may vary considerably but collecting the data from the whole class would give a more reliable set of results. An estimate of the number of packs needed to get a full set could be obtained by taking the average for the whole class.
- After the class have completed Task 1 they can do Task 2, which is essentially the same except that the number of different stickers in the set is changed, so that some of the stickers are harder to obtain. Once again, to save time, pre-printed cards could be used.
- Task 2 should indicate that if the number of one sort of sticker is limited then the number of packs needed to get a full set increases.
- Task 3 is a method of modelling any situation with x stickers sold in packs of y. It is not a true model as duplicate numbers (stickers) can occur within any pack, which is not the case in reality. However, it will indicate that, as the example shows, even with 20 stickers in a set, and five stickers in a pack, after 20 packs have been purchased – a total of 100 stickers – there is still not a complete set.

Plenary

- Discuss what the results of the tasks show.
- Can the number of packs needed be accurately predicted for any situation where the number of stickers in the set and the number of stickers in the pack vary?
- Can the spreadsheet used in Task 3 be used to analyse Tasks 1 and 2? (yes to Task 1 but no to Task 2)
- Students could do internet searches, for example, on 'panini stickers uk 2010', to obtain information on current packs, they could set up a spreadsheet to find how many packs are needed to obtain a full set.

Resources
Pupil Book page 54
A4 card
sets of prepared cards (optional, see Worksheet: Stickers)
scissors
computers
computer spreadsheet program
internet access

© HarperCollins*Publishers* 2009

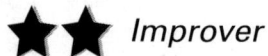 *Improver*

Outcomes

- Students will have used a mathematical model to analyse a real-life situation.
- Students will have used a spreadsheet to model a situation.
- Students will have worked cooperatively with others.

Answers

Task 3 (extension)

It is possible to model a situation where the number of printed stickers in the set varies.

The example below shows a situation where the set of 30 stickers contains one A, two Bs, three Cs, four Ds, five Es, six Fs and nine Gs, with stickers sold in packs of three. Even after 30 packs are sold there is no A.

To set up this spreadsheet enter the number of stickers in column E from 1 to the required number (in this case 30). In Column F enter the available stickers. This can be numerical or text.

In A1 enter the formula **=LOOKUP(INT(RAND()*30+1), $E$1:$E$30, $F$1:$F$30)**. Change the value 30 to suit the number of stickers.

Now copy this formula down and across. It should generate a series of letters or whatever was entered into column F.

The data can be analysed to see how many packs it takes to obtain a full set of stickers.

	A	B	C	D	E	F
1	E	C	E		1	A
2	E	B	E		2	B
3	C	F	C		3	B
4	E	E	G		4	C
5	C	E	F		5	C
6	E	F	B		6	C
7	G	D	D		7	D
8	G	G	F		8	D
9	D	G	D		9	D
10	F	C	C		10	D
11	C	E	D		11	E
12	F	D	G		12	E
13	E	C	G		13	E
14	E	C	D		14	E
15	F	G	E		15	E
16	F	G	F		16	F
17	F	G	C		17	F
18	C	G	C		18	F
19	D	G	C		19	F
20	G	B	G		20	F
21	G	E	E		21	F
22	D	F	G		22	G
23	F	G	G		23	G
24	C	G	F		24	G
25	E	D	C		25	G
26	F	B	G		26	G
27	D	E	B		27	G
28	E	F	F		28	G
29	E	G	D		29	G
30	D	D	E		30	G

Improver ★★

Worksheet: Stickers
Task 1

H	H	H	H
M	M	M	M
B	B	B	B
L	L	L	L
Mg	Mg	Mg	Mg

★★ *Improver*

Worksheet: Stickers
Task 2

H	H	M	M
M	B	B	B
B	L	L	L
L	L	Mg	Mg
Mg	Mg	Mg	Mg

© HarperCollins*Publishers* 2009

Money matters 4: Savings and AER

Context
- The activity is about interpreting information given in unfamiliar forms.
- It is a pre-requisite that students know how to work out a percentage of a quantity.

Lesson plan

Starter
- Start with a mental test on simple percentages, for example, ask students:
  - What is 10% of £500?
  - What is 5% of £5000?
  - What is 1% of £200?
- Students could use mini-whiteboards to give their answers.
- Now use the warm-up questions, giving answers as you go along.
- The warm-up questions do not compare accounts but simply make the students familiar with the way the accounts operate.

Main activity
- This activity involves students in comparing interest rates rather than calculating actual amounts of interest, although they will need to be able to do this for question 5 and Task 1.
- Tell students about the **annual equivalent rate** (AER), which is the interest rate quoted on interest paid on savings and investments. Explain that it is a fair way of comparing saving rates.
- Review how to calculate percentages of £500, £1000 and £5000 for various rates of interest, Use rates that are different from those given in the Pupil Book.
- Ask students to complete Task 1.
- Explain that some advertisements are easier to understand than others.
- Ask students to put the five advertisements in order of how easy they are to understand, starting with the easiest and finishing with the most difficult.
- Now ask students to look at Task 2. Explain that you want them to come up with a good advertisement of their own, using the best parts of those shown in the Pupil Book.

Plenary
- Ask students to tell you what they liked about the advertisements and what they did not like.
- Check if there is agreement between different groups.
- Let students present their advertisements and ask them to say why they are better than those given in the Pupil Book.

Learning objectives

Representing: recognise that a real-life problem can be solved using appropriate mathematics; decide how to show the initial problem using mathematical symbols

Analysing: establish a pattern or relationship and then change the variables to see how this changes the results

Interpreting: check that a conclusion is appropriate and accurate in the context of the original problem; give a conclusion or answer to the original problem, using language and forms of presentation that make sense to a wider population

Performing: use mathematical skills and knowledge to make progress on a problem, even if it does not use a routine mathematical procedure; use a range of mathematics to find solutions

APP: evidence for Using and applying mathematics, Calculating

PLTS: develops Independent enquirers, Self-managers

Cross-curricular links: ICT, English, Art

© HarperCollins*Publishers* 2009

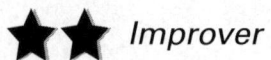 *Improver*

Extension work

- Ask students to sort the advertisements into order of best investment, starting with the one that offers poorest value.
- Compare results to find which investment was generally thought to be the best.
- If there is disagreement, discuss the reasons for this.
- Discuss the effects of making withdrawals and see how this affects their rank order.

Outcomes

- Students will have had opportunities to understand practical problems in unfamiliar contexts.
- Students will have identified information necessary to tackle the problem.
- Students will have applied mathematics to find solutions to practical problems and communicated solutions, drawing simple conclusions and giving explanations.

Underpinning maths: percentage of a quantity understanding of AER

Resources
Pupil Book page 57
mini-whiteboards
internet access

Answers

Warm-up questions

1.
   a. An investment for which the interest rate is fixed and the investment period is also fixed
   b. No, £5000 is the minimum investment
   c. £22.50
   d. £112.50

2.
   a. On the internet
   b. 2.50% gross AER
   c. 0.1% gross AER

3.
   a. £500
   b. 1.5% gross AER
   c. No penalty

4.
   a. £1000
   b. After 12 months, provided you have kept at least £1000 in the account

5.
   a. 180 day loss of interest on the amount withdrawn during the fixed-rate period
   b. £1
   c. The amount received after basic rate tax per year (per annum)

Shuffleboard

Context
- This activity is mainly about using the data-handling cycle.
- Shuffleboard is a popular game, mainly played on cruise ships, but there are many land-based clubs around the world, principally in North America.
- The game itself may not be familiar to many students; the rules are quite complex but, for the purposes of this task, they have been simplified.
- Players aim four discs in turn at triangular targets marked at each end of the playing area. A diagram of the playing area is shown in the Pupil Book and the dimensions can be found on the internet. These are not used in the task, although they could be used within extension work.

Lesson plan

Starter
- With the students, look at the diagram in the Pupil Book. Ask students if any of them have ever played shuffleboard. They may answer yes or they may have played a similar game that is based on a table. In either case establish that the aim of the game is to slide discs along the surface to land within scoring zones.
- The scoring triangle for **deck shuffleboard** is shown in the Pupil Book. This is drawn to scale so opportunities exist for extension work on area and scale drawing.
- The official dimensions of a shuffleboard court are measured in feet, so there are also opportunities for work on imperial and metric conversion.
- Briefly go through the rules, described above, which have been simplified so that a player's score consists of the total score of each of the four discs in play.
- The actual rules are far more complex and can be found on the internet but it is advisable to disregard them as they will probably confuse students.
- Make sure that students are aware that the **10 off** section represents a loss of 10 points.

Main activity
- There are three tasks. The first two are just warm-ups and involve nothing more than basic numeracy.
- Task 1 is a simple addition of scores;
- Task 2 is best done by students in small groups. The table is available on Worksheet: Shuffleboard.
- Task 3 is the main activity and requires students to find which of three people should be chosen for a team, based on previous performance.

Learning objectives

Representing: decide which methods to use to make progress with the solution

Analysing: establish a pattern or relationship and then change the variables to see how this changes the results; find a result or solution to the original problem

Interpreting: interpret results and solutions and make a generalisation about them; test generalisations and draw conclusions from the mathematical analysis

Performing: use a range of mathematics to find solutions; check work and methods when tacking a problem and decide if a different approach may be more effective

APP: evidence for Using and applying mathematics, Handling data

PLTS: develops Creative thinkers, Effective participators

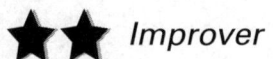 *Improver*

- It is worth discussing this task with students to make sure they have some idea how to make progress and what mathematics may be necessary.
- It is important for students to realise that if this question appeared in a Functional Mathematics paper it would be worth quite a few marks, possibly up to 6. In order to gain all the marks students would need to do a lot of relevant mathematics.
- On the other hand, any progress they make, even if it may not lead them to a correct conclusion, would score some marks.
- For this reason the mark scheme outlined below is not a straightforward 'right or wrong' but attempts to award students for use of relevant techniques and reasoning.

Plenary

Discuss the conclusions students have drawn.
- It is fairly obvious why Clara would be chosen. Her mean score (31.5) is much higher than those of the others. (22 each)
- The reserve could be either of Alf and Brenda. Their means are the same. Students should also be encouraged to look at how consistent they are with their scoring.
- Alf has a range of 27. Brenda has a range that could vary between 6 and 14 so she is the more consistent. On the other hand, Alf has five scores over 30 while Brenda has none.
- It would not matter what choice was made as long as the conclusion was backed up with evidence, using data from the table or the scores.
- Students should be encouraged to use the least well considered part of the data-handling cycle, which is **evaluating**. What could they do to make the choice more reliable? (Collect more data)
- What other measures could be used? (mode, median) What could have led to bias in the results? (Were data collected in competition or in practice?)

Outcomes

- Students will have worked with others to analyse a situation and reach a conclusion.
- Students will have used the data-handling cycle.

Answers

Task 1

a Red 23, yellow 15

b Red 30, yellow 34

c Red −5, yellow 29

Task 2

All scores apart from 9, 19, 29 and 39 are possible.

Underpinning maths:
basic numeracy
negative numbers
stem-and-leaf diagram
averages of discrete data
mean of a grouped table
range
comparison of distributions using one measure of location and one measure of spread

Resources
Pupil Book page 60
internet access
Worksheet:
Shuffleboard

© HarperCollins*Publishers* 2009

Improver

Task 3

Assume the question is worth 6 marks in total.

Mark	Criteria	Example
1	Student extracts any piece of data from any set of data. Or, extracts two pieces of data from any one set of data.	• Clara's mode is 34. • Alf has a lowest score of 7 and highest score of 34.
2	Student extracts any piece of data from at least two of the sets of data and makes a valid conclusion. Or, extracts two pieces of data from either of the two data sources and makes a valid comment about these.	• Clara's highest score is 40, but Alf's highest score is only 34. • Clara has a lot of scores in the 30s and some around 20. • Alf's range is 27 (range implies two pieces of data read). • Adds midpoint column to grouped table (implies two pieces of data).
3	Student calculates a mean for Alf **or** Clara. Or, writes down a mode for both Alf **and** Clara.	• Mean for Alf is 660 ÷ 30 = 22. • Mean for Clara is 1008 ÷ 32 = 31.5. • Mode for Alf = 28. • Mode for Clara = 34.
4	Student calculates the mean and range for Alf **and** Clara. Or, makes it clear that range for Brenda is between 14 and 6.	• Range for Alf = 27. • Range for Clara = 24. • Range for Brenda between 16 to 30 (14) and 20 to 26 (6).
5	Student calculates the mean of a grouped table using midpoint values.	• Midpoints are 18, 23 and 28. xf are 162, 414, 84. Σxf = 660.
6	Student calculates all means and ranges and reaches a valid conclusion for both parts of the question.	• Clara has the highest mean and few low scores. • Alf should be chosen as the reserve as he has a mean of 22 and scores a lot of scores over 30. • Brenda should be chosen as the reserve as she has a mean of 22 and is very consistent.

Task 4 (Extension)

Isosceles triangle: 3 square feet; two '8' trapezia, 4.5 square feet each; two '7' trapezia, 7.5 square feet each; rectangle 9 square feet

P(10) = 0.083, P(8) = 0.25, P(7) = 0.417, P(−10) = 0.25

© HarperCollins*Publishers* 2009

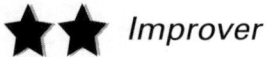

Worksheet: Shuffleboard

Task 2

Score	Disc 1	Disc 2	Disc 3	Disc 4
4	0	7	7	−10
5	0	7	8	−10
6	0	8	8	−10
7	0	0	0	7
8	0	0	0	8
9	Not possible			
10				
11				
12				
13				
14				
15				
16				
17				
18				
19				
20				
21				
22				
23				
24				
25				

Score	Disc 1	Disc 2	Disc 3	Disc 4
26				
27				
28				
29				
30				
31				
32				
33				
34				
35				
36				
37				
38	10	10	10	10
39	Not possible			
40	10	10	10	10

Money matters 5: Mortgages

Context
- The activity is about repayment mortgages and understanding how they work.
- It is also about the advantages and disadvantages of variable and fixed rate loans.

Lesson plan

Starter
- Start by asking students if they know what a mortgage is. Point out that the word is used specifically to mean a loan for buying a house.
- Tell students that you plan to buy a house for £100 000 and that you intend to borrow the money and pay it back monthly over 25 years.
- Ask students to tell you how many payments will be needed. (25 × 12 = 300)
- Ask students to write down how much they think you would need to pay each month. (varies according to interest rate but would be £377 for 1% interest rate, rising to £909 for 10% interest rate)

Main activity
- The main activity involves comparing different mortgages, different rates of interest, different amounts borrowed and different borrowing periods.
- Explain that there are lots of different types of mortgage and this is why lots of people get confused when looking for a mortgage.
- Tell the students that this activity is about the most popular type of mortgage, called a **repayment mortgage**.
- Explain that, when someone is buying a house, they will usually need a **deposit** as most banks will not lend the full amount. The remainder that is being borrowed is called the **mortgage sum** or **mortgage amount**. You may need to explain what a deposit is.
- Discuss how mortgages work. Someone borrows a sum to pay for the house; this is repaid monthly over a long period, usually up to 25 years.
- Explain that the longer the repayment period, the longer the money is borrowed so the more there will be to pay back in the end.
- Task 1 is designed to demonstrate to students the effects of increases in interest rate and lengthening the term of a mortgage. The questions are intended to test whether the students can interpret results from a table. Questions 9 and 10 require the students to combine information to obtain the answers. They will need practice at this type of question first.

Learning objectives
Representing: recognise that a real-life problem can be solved using appropriate mathematics; decide how to show the initial problem using mathematical symbols

Analysing: establish a pattern or relationship and then change the variables to see how this changes the results

Interpreting: check that a conclusion is appropriate and accurate in the context of the original problem; give a conclusion or answer to the original problem, using language and forms of presentation that make sense to a wider population

Performing: use mathematical skills and knowledge to make progress on a problem, even if it does not use a routine mathematical procedure; use a range of mathematics to find solutions

APP: evidence for Using and applying mathematics, Calculating

PLTS: develops Independent enquirers, Self-managers

Cross-curricular links: ICT

© HarperCollinsPublishers 2009

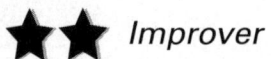 *Improver*

- Ask the students questions such as:
  - How could I use one of these table to work out different amounts of mortgage?
  - How could I work out the repayments for a mortgage of £220 000? (double £110 000)
- Now ask students to work through Task 1.
- Task 2 requires students to find and use an online mortgage calculator.
- If it is preferred, tell students which mortgage calculator to use.
- Explain to the students that the task is simply about getting them to familiarise themselves with the costs of borrowing and how repayments can change.
- Allow students to experiment with the calculator, with different variables.
- Ask students to summarise their findings.
- Task 3 could form part of the plenary. The compulsory warning may need explaining but is there to act as a reminder that there is a consequence for not keeping up with repayments.
- Let students be creative in designing their advertisements but remind them that information has to be clear and not misleading.

Extension work

- Ask students to find out about other types of mortgage that are available, for example, interest only or tracker, and how and why they are different.
- Ask students to make a list of other extra costs that would be involved in taking out a mortgage or buying a house, for example, deposit, insurance, payment protection, cost of fittings, furniture.
- Students could then feed back in groups to compile a composite list.

Plenary

- Ask students to say what they liked about the advertisements they studied, and what they did not like.
- Check if there is agreement between different groups.
- Let students present their own advertisements. Ask them to state the most important points and say why they are important.

Outcomes

- Students will have had experience in practical problems in an unfamiliar context.
- Students will have identified and obtained necessary information to tackle the problem.
- Students will have selected and applied mathematics in an organised way to find solutions and will have drawn simple conclusions and given explanations.

Underpinning maths: percentage of a quantity understanding of annual equivalent rate (AER)

Resources
Pupil Book page 64
computer
spreadsheet program
internet access
internet mortgage calculator

Time zones

Context

- Studying the time zone map in detail reveals that the limits of time zones are irregular. They take into account factors such as ensuring that the whole country (or region) is in the same time zone. Africa is a good example of a continent broken into irregular time zones.
- This can lead to much discussion or internet searches. There are many calculators on the internet that can be used to check time zones.
- Daylight saving times are used in many countries, not just Britain. This can be a confusing concept.
- This activity provides an opportunity to discuss whether time travel is possible. If you could move around the Earth faster than the Sun appears to move across the sky (approximately 1000 miles per hour), you could appear to travel back in time.
- The concept of there being different times in different places around the world is important, especially in relation to worldwide business and inter-continental travel. Most students will have heard of – or even have experienced – jet lag, which occurs when the body clock is out of synch with local time.

Lesson plan

Starter

- Start by asking students if they have travelled abroad.
- Many will have done this, so ask what they found different. Likely responses are language, food and weather but press students to mention time, particularly if the trip was to the USA.
- Ask students if they know why time is different around the world. Animations can be found on the internet. (Either do this before the lesson, or suggest that students try some research.)
- Explain that the Earth makes one rotation on its axis every 24 hours. Local time is set according to when the Sun reaches its highest point each day, which is midday or noon.
- Ask students to imagine a point on the equator (the imaginary line around the Earth, perpendicular to its axis, at its widest point). This point will take a full day to move one rotation.
- Therefore the point will travel 1/24 of the circumference of the Earth in 1 hour. This distance is equivalent to a rotation of 360° ÷ 24 = 15°. This is why time zones are 15° of longitude wide.
- Make sure students know that the Earth is tilted on its axis, relative to the plane of its orbit around the Sun.
- Discuss why, in terms of hours of daylight, days are shorter in the winter and longer in the summer.
- If internet access is available ask students to research reasons for time being standardised through the world. Otherwise go through the basics of UTC, GMT and daylight saving, as mentioned in the Pupil Book.

Learning objectives

Representing: recognise that a real-life problem can be solved, using appropriate mathematics

Analysing: find a result or solution to the original problem

Interpreting: give a conclusion or answer to the original problem, using language and forms of presentation that make sense to a wider population

Performing: give a solution to a practical problem, even if it is not within a familiar context and make sure the solution is presented in a clear and understandable way

APP: evidence for Calculating

PLTS: develops Independent enquirers

Cross-curricular links: Science, ICT, Geography

Underpinning maths:
clock times
addition of times
subtraction of times

© HarperCollins*Publishers* 2009

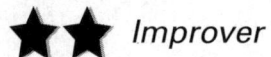 *Improver*

Main activity

- Show a screen shot of a flight from London to New York, for example:

| **08:20** Depart London (LHR)
Arrive New York (JFK) **11:55** | Tue 20 Jan
Duration: 8 hours 35 min | TransUniverse Airlines
Direct flight | 3554 |
| **08:55** Depart New York (JFK)
Arrive London (LHR) **21:15** | Tue 3 Feb
Duration: 7 hours 20 min | TransUniverse Airlines
Direct flight | 3555 |

Resources
Pupil Book page 67
atlas
graph paper
internet access (optional)
Worksheet: Time zones

- Discuss the times shown.
  If the flight leaves at 08:20 and takes 8 hours 35 minutes, it would land at 16:55 London time but it lands at 11:55 local time
- Ask what the time difference is.
- Look at the Pupil Book. Work through the following examples.

Example 1

A flight takes off from Karachi for New York. The plane leaves Karachi at 08:00 local time. The flight takes 13 hours and 15 minutes. What is the local time when it lands in New York?

Answer

Karachi is UTC + 5 and New York is UTC − 5 so the time difference is 10 hours. That means that the plane takes off at 10 pm the day before, New York time. Adding 13 hours and 15 minutes to this gives 11:15 as the landing time.

Example 2

Three schools in Norway (UTC + 1), England (UTC + 0) and Dallas (UTC − 6) form a link. The school in Norway is open from 10 am to 5 pm. The school in England is open from 9 am to 3.30 pm. The school in Dallas is open from 7 am to 2.30 pm. During what local time in England can the three schools video-conference with each other?

Answer

Convert all the opening times to local time in England.

School in Norway is open from 9 am to 4 pm local time in England.

School in Dallas is open from 1 pm to 8.30 pm local time in England.

School in England is open from 9 am to 3.30 pm.

This gives an overlap of 1 pm to 3.30 pm, which is when a video conference could take place.

- Students can now do the questions in the Pupil Book. If extra support is required for questions 7 and 8, students can be provided with Worksheet: Time zones.

Plenary

- Ask students if they have friends or family in other countries and discuss when is the best time to call them.
- You could call out countries where family and friends live and ask students when you should call them.

Improver

Outcomes
- Students will have solved a practical problem that is not within a familiar context.
- Students will have made sure the solution is presented in a clear and understandable way.

Answers

1. 10 am
2. 4 pm
3. 20 h 30 min
4. 4 hours (1 pm to 5 pm)
5. 8 pm
6. 4.30 pm
7. London: 6 pm, Los Angeles: 10 am, Moscow: 9 pm, Karachi: 11 pm
8. AU1: 12:55; AU2: 12:30; AU3: 8 h 20 m; AU4: 9 h 30 m; AU5: 07:15
9. Andrew: 12:55; Carol: 07:55
10. 12 midday and 2 pm

★★ *Improver*

Worksheet: Time zones

7

New York   London   Los Angeles   Moscow   Karachi

8

Flight	Destination	Departure	Length of flight	Arrival Time
AU1	Moscow	06:45	3 h 10 m	
AU2	Paris	10:25	1 h 05 m	
AU3	New York	11:10		14:30
AU4	Los Angeles	08:50		10:20
AU5	Karachi		8 h 15 m	20:30

Planning a bedroom

Context
- The lesson is about planning and making sensible decisions.

Lesson plan

Starter
- Ask students to look at the Data sheet: Planning a bedroom.
- Prompt them to explain the difference between the measurements **depth**, **width** and **height**.
- Check that students can convert between millimetres, centimetres and metres.
- Point out that the bed sizes are given in centimetres but the wardrobes and drawers are given in millimetres, whereas the scale given on the tasks is in metres.
- Test the students' capabilities in converting units by asking them to make relevant conversions, for example, 'How many metres is 900 mm?'

Main activity
- Explain that the three planning tasks are for bedrooms of different sizes.
- In each case the first decision is whether to make it into a double room or a single room.
- Discuss which pieces of furniture can go under a window and which would not fit. It may be worth saying that the bottom of all windows in the bedrooms in these plans is 1 metre above the floor level.
- Point out that, in general, men need more drawers than women but women need more wardrobe space because of the different types of clothing.
- It may help if students make plan-view cut-outs of their furniture to experiment on their graph paper before making the final drawings.
- To complete each task, the students will need to have completed accurate scale drawings, each showing a bed (or two singles), wardrobes and drawers or other storage space.
- It must be possible to open doors fully and, depending on the ability of the group, some access will be needed to the windows.
- Students are also asked to produce a brief report, giving clear reasons for every decision taken.
- Students who finish the task quickly could design two plans for each bedroom and then include in their report the advantages and disadvantages for each design.

Learning objectives

Representing: recognise that a real-life problem can be solved using appropriate mathematics

Analysing: use appropriate mathematical procedures; find a result or solution to the original problem

Interpreting: check that a conclusion is appropriate and accurate in the context of the original problem; give a conclusion or answer to the original problem, using language and forms of presentation that make sense to a wider population

Performing: use mathematical skills and knowledge to make progress on a real-life problem, even if the situation described is not within a familiar context; check work and methods when tackling a problem and decide if a different approach may be more effective

APP: evidence for Using and applying mathematics

PLTS: develops Creative thinkers, Self-managers

Cross-curricular links: Design and technology, ICT

© HarperCollins*Publishers* 2009

 *Advanced*

Plenary

- Students should display their plans and discuss other possible features that have not been included in the basic task, for example, using part of an L-shape room as an en-suite bathroom or moving the position of doors to facilitate the better arrangement of the room.

Extension work

- Students could redesign their own bedrooms, using internet searches or furniture brochures to choose colour schemes or wood types.
- Alternatively, they could use internet searches to find prices of beds and bedroom furniture, and then calculate or estimate the cost of their plans.

Outcomes

- Students will have made sure the solution is presented in a clear and understandable way.
- Students will have used mathematics to gain insight into a real-life problem.
- Students will have understood a practical problem in a familiar context.
- Students will have communicated situations and reasoning.

Underpinning maths:
scale drawing
measuring

Resources
Pupil Book page 71
centimetre-squared graph paper
internet access
Data sheet: Planning a bedroom

© HarperCollins*Publishers* 2009

Data sheet: Planning a bedroom

Advanced ★★★

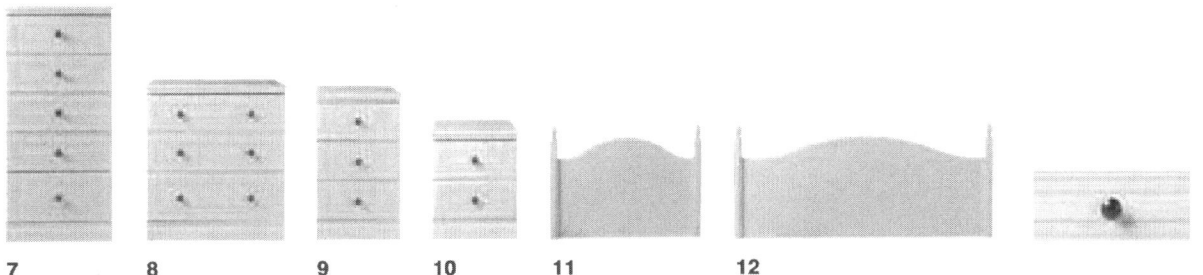

1.	3 door mirror wardrobe*	H1873 x W1141x D525mm	5017860716557	£400
2.	2 door wardrobe	H1873 x W760 x D525mm	5017860716496	£250
3.	2 door combi wardrobe	H1873 x W760 x D525mm	5017860716335	£300
4.	Dressing table	H759 x W972 x D406mm	5017860716458	£275
5.	5 drawer wide chest	H1027 x W766 x D406mm	5017860716373	£225
6.	7 drawer wide chest	H822 x W1147 x D406mm	5017860716618	£275
7.	5 drawer tall chest	H822 x W1147 x D406mm	5017860716397	£225
8.	3 drawer wide chest	H822 x W766 x D406mm	5017860716359	£200
9.	3 drawer bedside chest	H759 x W450 x D406mm	5017860716472	£125
10.	2 drawer bedside chest	H554 x W448 x D406mm	5017860716311	£100
11.	Single headboard	H587 x W914 x D70mm	5017860716410	£100
12.	Double Headboard	H587 x W1524 x D70mm	5017860716434	£150

Everything here is ready-assembled* and delivered direct to your home.

* With the exception of the 3 door wardrobes which are flat-packed for self-assembly to allow access into your home.

Bed sizes

small single	75 cm x 190 cm	double	135 cm x 190 cm
single	90 cm x 190 cm	king	150 cm x 200 cm
super single	105 cm x 190 cm	super king	180 cm x 200 cm
three-quarter (small double)	120 cm x 190 cm		

© HarperCollins*Publishers* 2009

Stopping distances

Context
- Students are unlikely to be totally familiar with this context, although they will have some idea about road safety and the dangers of excessive speed.
- Some sensitivity may be needed if any students or their relatives have recently been involved in a road accident but the activity does present an excellent opportunity to emphasise a road-safety measure.

Lesson plan

Starter
- It is advised to distribute Data sheet: Stopping distances at least a day before the lesson and ask students to think about some questions that could be asked from it.
- An article from the local paper about a recent crash could provide an effective introduction. It could also be used as a starting point for a discussion.
- Ask students to look at the data sheet and prepare at least one question that could be asked, based on the data.
- If necessary generate some discussion on aspects such as total stopping distance. The graphs need some interpretation and may need explaining, particularly the graph about the probability of a fatality.

Main activity
- Start by asking students what questions they thought of, based on the chart showing thinking and braking distances. Discuss their questions and answer them if possible.
- When students are familiar with interpreting the data in the chart they can do Task 1.
- Task 2 uses a road safety table from the US to introduce new data. Look at the table with the students and discuss what it means.
- In many states in the US the speed limit is 75 mph, which is why the table goes up in steps of 10 mph from 25 mph. Explain how to find average values to work out the distances for in-between values such as 30 mph.
- Let students do Task 2.
- Ask students what questions they thought of, based on the two graphs showing emergency braking from 60 mph. Discuss their questions and answer them if possible.
- When students are familiar with interpreting the graphs they can do Task 3.

Learning objectives

Representing: recognise that a real-life problem can be solved using appropriate mathematics

Analysing: analyse a pattern or a relationship, using appropriate techniques

Interpreting: interpret results and solutions and make a generalisation about them

Performing: use mathematical skills and knowledge to make progress on a real-life problem, even if the situation described is not within a familiar context; use a range of mathematics to find solutions

APP: evidence for Algebra, Calculating

PLTS: develops Independent enquirers, Creative thinkers

Cross-curricular links: ICT, English

Underpinning maths:
distance, time, speed
drawing and interpretation of graphs
conversion between linear metric and imperial units
probability

© HarperCollins*Publishers* 2009

Advanced

Plenary

- Discuss with students what they have learned from doing this task.
- They should have a much better grasp of road safety issues and safe speeds.
- In particular, ask about the speed at which risk of fatality becomes almost zero (30 mph) and relate this to the speed limit in built-up areas.
- Discuss with students the advantages and disadvantages of reducing the speed limit to 20 mph outside schools when students are present. This relates to the suggested extension task.

Outcomes

- Students will have used mathematics to gain insight into a real-life problem.
- Students will have interpreted graphs.
- Students will have drawn a graph by linking two variables via a third variable.

Resources

Pupil Book page 74
local news clippings about road traffic accidents
graph paper
internet access
Data sheet: Stopping distances
Worksheet: Stopping distances

Answers

Task 1

1. 16
2. 15 m
3. 55 m
4. 36 m
5. 96 m
6. 13.5 m
7. 84.5 m
8. 24
9.
10. See the graph opposite; thinking: 24 m: braking: about 86 m; total: about 110 m.

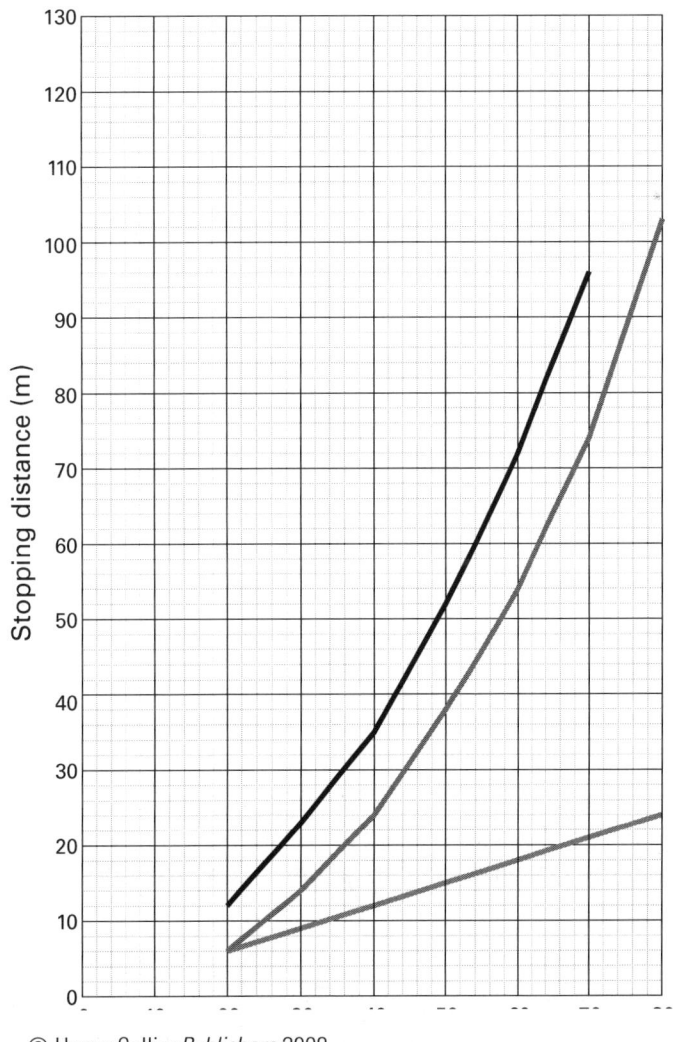

 *Advanced*

Task 2

1.

Speed (mph)	30	40	50	60	70
3-second (ft)	138.5	182	220.5	265.5	310.5
6-second (ft)	267	354	441	531	621

2.

Speed (mph)	30	40	50	60	70
3-second (ft)	43	56	68	82	96
6-second (ft)	82	109	136	163	191

3. At the lowest speed the US table advises about double the UK distance, but they get closer as the speed increases and they agree at 70 mph.

4.

Speed (mph)	30	40	50	60	70
Formula (feet)	75	120	175	240	315
Formula (m)	23	37	54	74	97
Chart	23	36	53	73	96

The formula agrees with the chart to within 1 metre.

Task 3

1. 120 ft
2. 2 s
3. a 30 mph
   b 100 ft
   c 1.5 s
4. 0.25 s
5. 30 mph
6. 100 ft
7. 0.25 s
8. 75 ft
9. 12 mph
10. Emergency braking from 60 mph

Emergency braking from 60 mph

Task 4 (extension)

You should point out that the risk of a fatality is 0.25 at 30 mph, is 0.16 at 20 mph and that schools can be busy at certain times of the day with students crossing roads and not paying attention as they meet their friends.

Data sheet: Stopping distances

This table shows the **thinking distance** and **braking distance** for a driver to react and stop in an emergency.

The **thinking distance** is the distance the car travels **while the driver's brain reacts**; this is before the driver starts to apply the brake to the car.

The **braking distance** is the distance the car will travel before it comes to a stop.

The **braking distance** is approximate and represents a **maximum**. In reality, the braking distance may be less.

One **car length** is **4 metres** so at **20 mph** the total **braking distance** is **12 metres** or **3 car lengths**.

It would therefore be sensible for a driver to leave **3 car lengths** between their car and the car in front to be sure that there is sufficient distance to think and brake in an emergency.

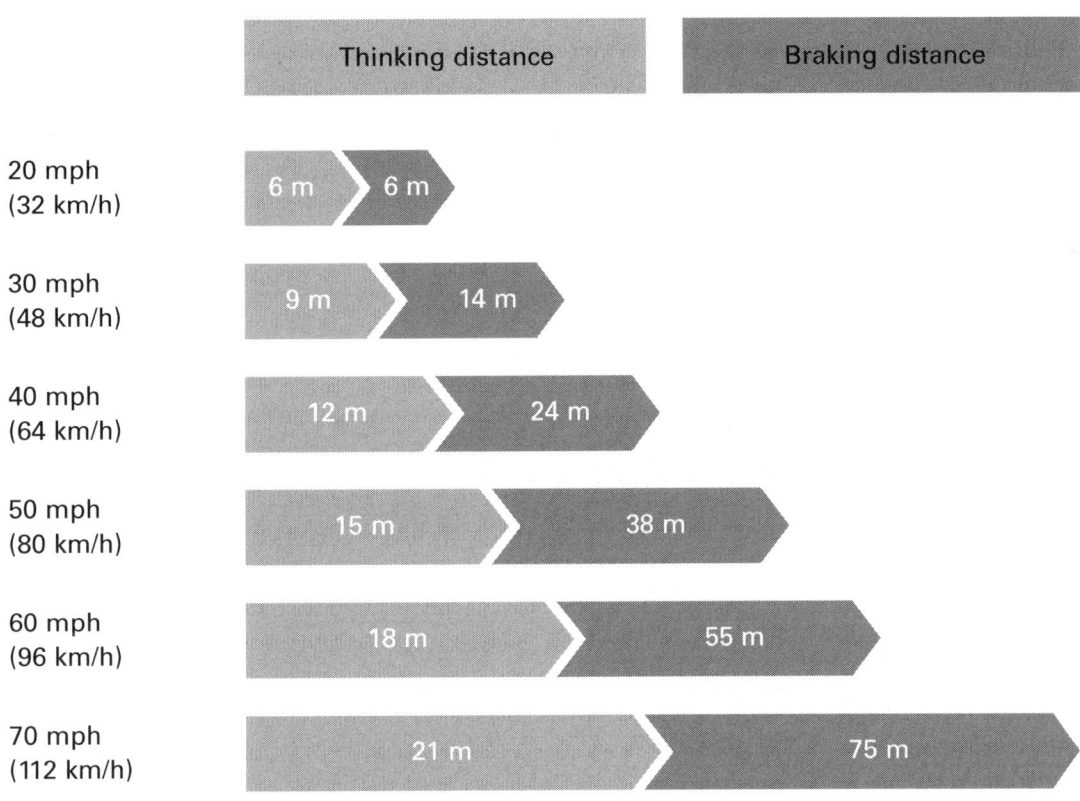

Speed	Thinking distance	Braking distance
20 mph (32 km/h)	6 m	6 m
30 mph (48 km/h)	9 m	14 m
40 mph (64 km/h)	12 m	24 m
50 mph (80 km/h)	15 m	38 m
60 mph (96 km/h)	18 m	55 m
70 mph (112 km/h)	21 m	75 m

© HarperCollins*Publishers* 2009

Advanced

Emergency braking from 60 mph

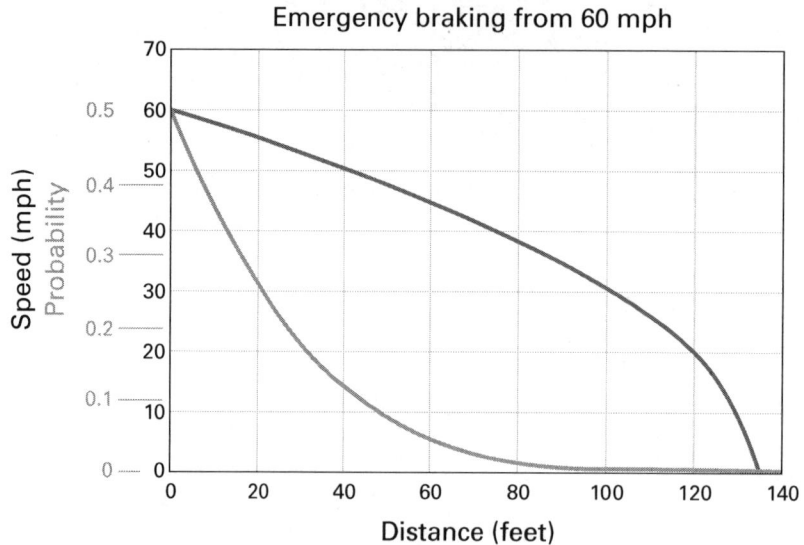

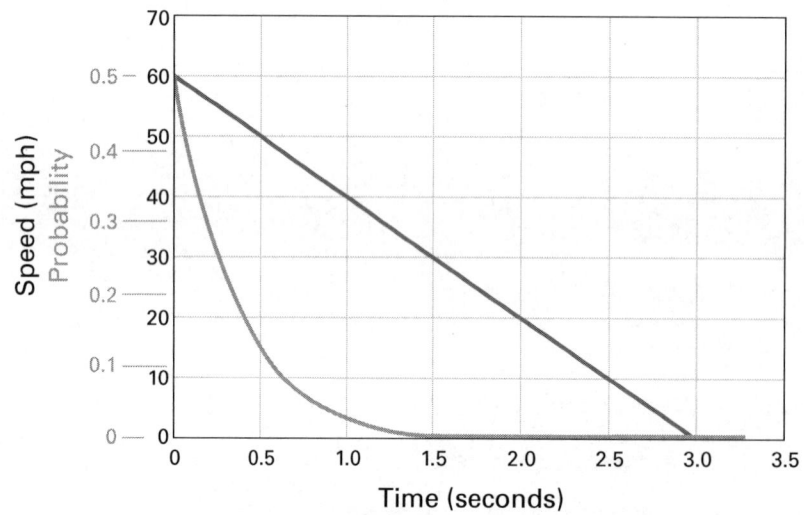

© HarperCollins*Publishers* 2009

Worksheet: Stopping distances

Task 1
9

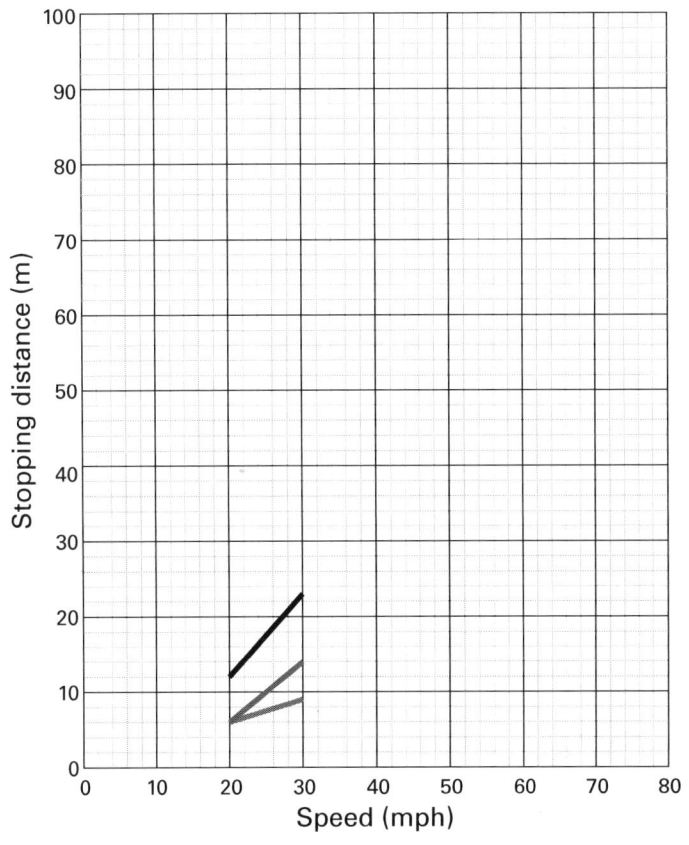

Task 3
10

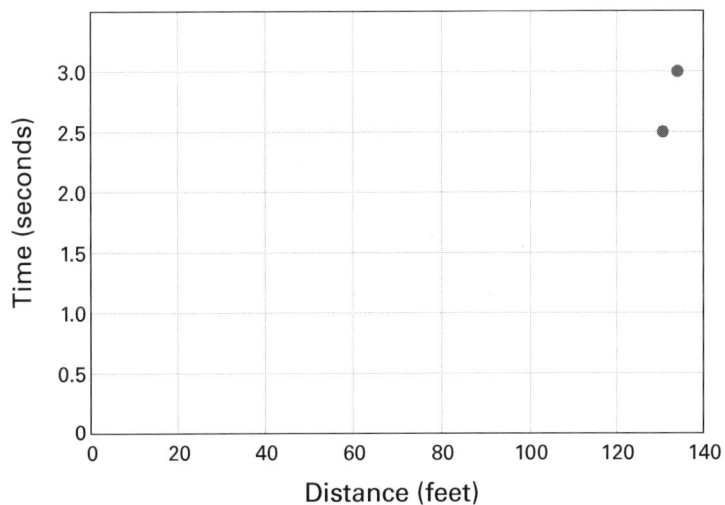

Climate change

Context
- This activity is about accessing data and presenting reports, using mathematics to support any views expressed.

Lesson plan

Starter
- Show students the first graph about carbon dioxide levels and ask them to read off different values, for example:
  - How many parts per million of carbon dioxide were there in the atmosphere in 1850, 1900, 1950 and 2000?
  - What is the trend?
- Now look with students at the first temperature-change graph and ask them to read off different values, for example:
  - What was the temperature change from the mean temperature in 1850, 1900, 1950 and 2000?
  - What is the trend?
- Now look at the graphs for the last 400 000 years. Ask the students to describe any patterns.
- Encourage students to put a timescale on their answers, for example, for carbon dioxide the pattern repeats about every 80 000 years.

Main activity
- Explain that in this activity students will be using information about climate change to look for patterns in data or to predict future trends.
- Task 1 could be done as a group discussion, with students then writing a short report of their findings. Ask students to look at the graphs as a pair and compare the shapes.
- Students should see that the patterns are similar: as concentration of carbon dioxide increases, so does the temperature change.
- Task 2 is intended to test students' mathematics skills within this context.
- Check that students are able to work out percentages of quantities as this is needed for question 5.
- Check also that students can express one quantity as a percentage of another, as this is required for question 8.
- Students can now complete Task 2.
- Encourage students to look carefully at the facts and predictions for Task 2 in order to help them complete Task 3.
- In preparation for Task 3, explain that, while many people think climate change is a problem brought about by human behaviour, others believe that it is just part of a long-term cycle.

Learning objectives

Representing: decide how to represent the problem to make it easier to solve using mathematics

Analysing: use appropriate mathematical procedures

Interpreting: test generalisations and draw conclusions from the mathematical analysis

Performing: check work and methods when tackling a problem and decide if a different approach may be more effective

APP: evidence for Using and applying mathematics, Handling data

PLTS: develops Creative thinkers

Cross-curricular links: ICT, Science, Geography

Underpinning maths:
interpreting graphs
time series graphs
percentages
fractions
number work

Resources
Pupil Book page 78
graph paper
internet access

Advanced

- Ask students to give reasons why the graphs can be used to support either viewpoint, for example, on the second pair of graphs the trend or cycle has been happening over hundreds of years and people did not produce the vast amounts of carbon dioxide from cars until about the last 100 years. However, on the first pair of graphs, the increase is quite dramatic and suggests this is not part of a long-term trend.

Plenary

- Go through the answers for Task 2 to check students' understanding

Extension work

- Ask students to research climate change or global warming further. They could use internet searches to do this.
- They could, for example, concentrate on one area such as finding information about landfill targets.

Outcomes

- Students will have used mathematics to gain insight into a real-life problem.
- Students will have extracted information from graphs.
- Students will have interpreted graphs.
- Students will have used basic mathematics to get insight into a everyday topic that affect us at the local and global level.

Answers

Task 2

1. 90 years
2. 7 years
3. 434 000 000
4. 0.5 metres
5. 300 million
6. 21.9 million
7. $\frac{9}{10}$
8. 0.01%

© HarperCollins*Publishers* 2009

Growing, growing, grown...

Context
- The topic of the activity is exponential growth.
- Students do not often grasp the speed at which things can grow exponentially.
- The activity leads fairly quickly into four practical or investigative problems. Although these are not all functional mathematics, they will give students practice in process and problem-solving skills.

Lesson plan

Starter
- Any starting activities that encourage students to think about exponential growth are useful, as would be some work on powers.
- Start by asking the classic puzzle: 'If a water lily doubles in size each day and takes 30 days to cover a pond completely, how many days did it take to cover half the pond?' The majority of students will answer 15 days. If any responds with 29 days, ask them to explain this (correct) answer.
- Another slightly simpler starter would be to ask students to count on by doubling a number, either as a group or individually; for example, starting with 2, ask them to generate a series by doubling. You may find some starting 2, 4, 6,... as they do not realise that every term after the first is double the previous term. Keep going until the calculations become too difficult or, if counting as a group, the series breaks down. This will be easy to spot as there will be a lot of wrong answers or mumbling as students lose track of the series.
- The Pupil Book suggests a practical starter. Give each student a sheet of thin paper or a tissue. Ask them to fold their paper in half as many times as possible. They may manage six folds in total but it is unlikely they will get a sharp fold the seventh time.
- Explain that they are trying to fold twice the number of layers each time so by the sixth fold they are trying to fold 64 layers.
- Finally, refer to the problem outlined in the Pupil Book. If an infinitely large piece of paper is cut and stacked so that the number of layers doubles each time, how high would the pile be after 50 cuts?
- Ask students for their estimates. Most will say a few metres at best. The answer is **112 million kilometres**. This can be explained in the plenary.

Main activity
- Ask students to state the **square** numbers.
- Ask how these are represented.
- Repeat with the **cube** numbers. They may need calculators to work out some of the later cubes.
- This will lead to the concept of **powers**.
- Remind students about **power notation**. There are two examples in the Pupil Book.

Learning objectives

Representing: decide which methods to use to make progress with the solution; decide how to represent the problem to make it easier to solve using mathematics

Analysing: analyse a pattern or a relationship, using appropriate techniques

Interpreting: interpret results and solutions and make a generalisation about them; test generalisations and draw conclusions from the mathematical analysis

Performing: give a solution to a practical problem, even if it is not within a familiar context, and make sure the solution is presented in a clear and understandable way; draw a conclusion from working and provide a mathematical justification for this conclusion

APP: evidence for Using and applying mathematics, Calculating

PLTS: develops Self-managers, Reflective learners

Cross-curricular links: ICT

© HarperCollins*Publishers* 2009

Advanced

Underpinning maths:
square numbers
powers
estimation
fractions

Resources
Pupil Book page 81
internet access
Worksheet: Growing, growing, grown…

- Depending on the ability of the group, you may choose to talk through some of the questions in the exercise. The diagrams are presented on Worksheet: Growing, growing, grown… Question 5, in particular, could require some planning and breaking down to make the problem more manageable.
- Questions 1 and 2 are just warm-up exercises on powers. Question 2 introduces negative powers. Some introductory work on these could be done, although students should be familiar with tenths, hundredths, etc.
- Students may find Question 3 easier if they use the worksheet. Alternatively, if it is done as a class activity, display a copy of the maze at the front for them to fill in numbers as the balls drop through. This can then be extended to fractions with half ($\frac{1}{2}$) going to either side. As the balls progress through the maze, the fractions that 'meet' are added together, giving $\frac{1}{2}, \frac{1}{2}$ at A, $\frac{1}{4}, \frac{2}{4}, \frac{1}{4}$ at BC, $\frac{1}{8}, \frac{3}{8}$, $\frac{3}{8}, \frac{1}{8}$ at DEF and $\frac{1}{16}, \frac{4}{16}, \frac{6}{16}, \frac{4}{16}, \frac{1}{16}$ at GHIJ. An extension activity linked to this is **Pascal's triangle**.
- For Question 4, students will need to be able to use the power button on their calculators. Before they start this question, ask students for an estimate for parts a and b. Some calculators may give answers in **standard form**. This may need to be explained.
- Question 5 provides an opportunity to reinforce problem-solving. Breaking the problem down leads to a fairly obvious series. A nice way to set out the results is in a table such as the one below (provided on Worksheet: Growing, growing, grown…). This should make the series of square numbers easy to identify.

Square	1 x 1	2 x 2	3 x 3	4 x 4	5 x 5	6 x 6	7 x 7	8 x 8	Total
1 x 1	1								1
2 x 2	4	1							5
3 x 3	9	4	1						14
4 x 4	16	9	4	1					30
5 x 5	25	16	9	4	1				55
6 x 6	36	25	16	9	4	1			91
7 x 7	49	36	25	16	9	4	1		140
8 x 8	64	49	36	25	16	9	4	1	204

- This could be extended by asking how big a board would be needed to give at least 1000 squares. (14 x 14 gives 1015 squares)
- Question 6 is just a calculation, albeit a complex one. The main point to make clear to students is that the number of grains of rice on previous squares must be included in the total. The number of grains is the series 1, 2, 4, … which is $2^0, 2^1, 2^2, …$ so the final square has 2^{63} grains on it. The total number of grains of rice is the sum of the series 1, 3, 7, 15, …
    - More able students may see that each term in this series is one less than the number of grains of rice on the next square.

© HarperCollins*Publishers* 2009

 *Advanced*

- This leads to the power series for the total number of grains as $2^1 - 1$, $2^2 - 1$, $2^3 - 1$, $2^4 - 1$, ... so the total by the time the final square is added is $2^{64} - 1$.
- The answer for the given values is shown below but you may want to find current values on the internet.
- Less able students may have trouble with conversions and the correct method of calculation. For some students, working through the answer will help.

Plenary

- Refer back to the problem posed at the start of the lesson. If a piece of paper is cut in half and the pieces stacked together and this is repeated 50 times how high will the resulting stack be? Ask students if they wish to revise their original estimates.
- Now work through the answer.
- A ream (500 sheets) of 80 g/m² paper is approximately 5 cm deep. This makes each sheet $\frac{1}{100}$ cm thick.
- After 1 cut there are 2 sheets (2^1), after 2 cuts there are 4 sheets (2^2) so after 50 cuts there are 2^{50} ($\approx 1.125 \times 10^{15}$) sheets.
- These are $1.125 \times 10^{15} \times \frac{1}{100}$ cm high = 1.125×10^{13} cm
- These are $1.125 \times 10^{13} \div 100$ metres high = 1.125×10^{11}
- These are $1.125 \times 10^{11} \div 1000 = 1.125 \times 10^8 \approx 112$ million kilometres high, which is almost all the way to the Sun!

Outcomes

- Students have an awareness of exponential growth.
- Students will know the powers of 10 for 100 to a million and for a tenth and a hundredth.
- Students will be confident with powers and the power keys on their calculators.
- Students will be able to interpret calculator displays for very large numbers.
- Students will have developed problem-solving skills.

Answers

1. **a** Increasing powers of 3 up to 3^9. Values are: 1, 3, 9, 27, 81, 243, 729, 2187, 6561

    b Increasing powers of 5 up to 5^9. Values are: 1, 5, 25, 125, 625, 3125, 15 625, 78 125, 390 625

    c Increasing calculations up to 3×2^9. Values are 3, 6, 12, 24, 48, 96, 192, 384, 768, 1536

2. 0.001, 10, 1000, 10 000; $\frac{1}{10000}$, $\frac{1}{100}$, $\frac{100}{1}$, $\frac{1000}{1}$, $\frac{10000}{1}$; 10^{-4}, 10^{-2},

3. **a** First level at A: 32 each side; second level: 16, 32 (16 + 16), 16; third level: 8, 24 (8 + 16), 24 (16 + 8), 8; fourth level: 4, 16 (4 + 12), 24 (12 + 12), 16 (12 + 4), 4

    b Tray 1: 4, tray 3: 24, tray 4: 16, tray 5: 4

4. **a** $2^{25} \approx 33\,500\,000$, $2^{26} \approx 67\,000\,000$, so on about 26 or 27 January.

    b $2^{32} \approx 4\,300$ million, $2^{33} \approx 8\,600$ million so about 3 or 4 February. Well before Valentine's day.

Advanced ★★★

5 The number of squares builds up as square numbers (see table in main lesson) to give a final total of 204. (See main lesson activity.)

6 The man's weight in grams is $80 \times 1000 = 80\,000$

The man's value in pounds is $80\,000 \times 22 = £1\,760\,000$

The total number of grains is $2^{64} - 1 \approx 1.845 \times 10^{19}$

This number of grains will weigh $1.845 \times 10^{19} \div 60\,000 = 3.075 \times 10^{14}$ kg

This weight of rice is $3.075 \times 10^{14} \div 1000 = 3.075 \times 10^{11}$ tonnes.

This weight of rice will cost $3.075 \times 10^{11} \times 700 = £2.1525 \times 10^{14}$

This is approximately £200 000 000 000 000 or 200 million million (200 trillion) pounds.

It looks like the old man got the better deal.

Task 1 (extension)

The Fibonacci sequence is formed by adding the two previous terms to get the next term.

It takes 17 terms to get over 1000. The 16th term is 987, the 17th is 1597.

Dividing subsequent terms leads to 1.618…, which is called the **Golden ratio**.

In nature Fibonacci occurs in seashells, seed heads and the growth of rabbit colonies.

© HarperCollins*Publishers* 2009

★★★ *Advanced*
Worksheet: Growing, growing, grown...

1 **a** 3^0 3^1 3^2 3^3 3^4 ...   .
         1   3   9   ...   .
   b 5^0 5^1 5^2 5^3 5^4 ...   .
         1   5   25   ...   .
   c 3×2^0 3×2^1 3×2^2 3×2^3 3×2^4 ...   .
         3   6   12   ...   .

2

Number	0.0001	0.01	0.1	1		100		
Fraction		$\frac{1}{100}$	$\frac{1}{10}$	1	$\frac{10}{1}$			
Power		10^{-3}		10^{-1}	10^0	10^1	10^2	10^3	10^4

3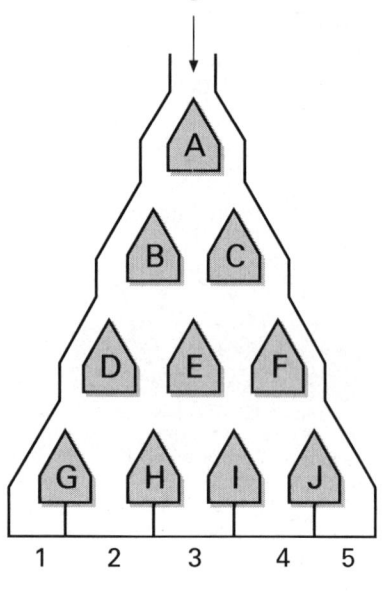

4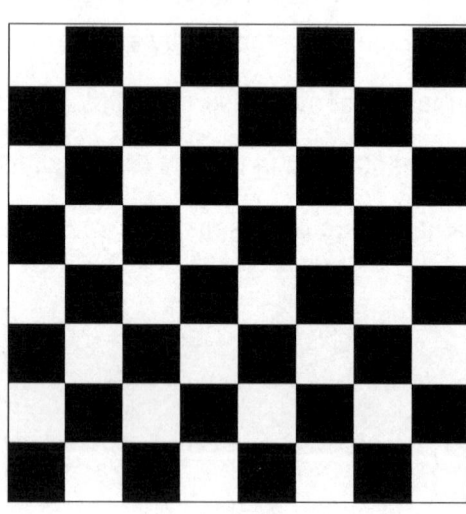

5

Square	1 x 1	2 x 2	3 x 3	4 x 4	5 x 5	6 x 6	7 x 7	8 x 8	Total
1 x 1	1								1
2 x 2	4	1							5
3 x 3	9	4	1						14
4 x 4									
5 x 5									
6 x 6									
7 x 7									
8 x 8									

© HarperCollins*Publishers* 2009

Recipes

Context
- This is a very open-ended activity.
- The difficulty is to ensure that the students include mathematics in their working rather than talking in general terms about the recipes.

Lesson plan

Starter
- Look at the recipes and ask the students to spot any obvious differences. They should realise that one recipe is for six people and the other is for eight people.
- Check that students are aware of the different numbers of servings, otherwise they might compare quantities of ingredients without taking this into account.
- Ask students to give some related facts, for example, ask questions such as:
  - What is the guideline daily amount of salt for a child aged seven?
  - What is the actual amount of salt in one serving of recipe 2?
- Point out that other ingredients may also contain salt.

Main activity
- This task is probably most successful if the students work in small groups.
- Explain the task to the students.
- Depending on the ability of the group, it may be necessary to instruct them to start by scaling the recipes to make them both serve 12 people.
- Students might try to cost each recipe but it would also be valid to state that, as the ingredients are similar, the costs might not vary much so the main comparison could be to check which caters for healthier eating.
- Explain that their report will have to contain some calculations and some valid comparisons.
- In the report they will also need to compare the guideline daily amounts for men, women and children.
- Students should also compare preparation and cooking times.
- It might be useful to give students a checklist of items for comparison.
- Point out that the nutrition information is per serving.

Learning objectives

Representing: decide which methods to use to make progress with the solution

Analysing: use appropriate mathematical procedures

Interpreting: interpret results and solutions and make a generalisation about them

Performing: analyse the situation or problem and decide which is the appropriate mathematical method needed to tackle it; give a solution to a practical problem, even if it is not within a familiar context, and make sure the solution is presented in a clear and understandable way

APP: evidence for Using and applying mathematics, Numbers and the number system

PLTS: develops Reflective thinkers, Self-managers

Cross-curricular links: ICT, Food Technology, Science

Underpinning maths:
scaling quantities
using proportions
costing items
finding best value

© HarperCollins*Publishers* 2009

 *Advanced*

Checklist
- [ ] Scale recipes so they are for same number of people, for example, 12 or 1.
- [ ] Compare the cost.
- [ ] Compare the ingredients, for example, which recipe has more fat?
- [ ] Compare the guideline daily amounts for men, women and children commenting if either recipe has too much of anything, bearing in mind this is only one part of one meal.
- [ ] Compare preparation times.
- [ ] Compare cooking times.
- [ ] Make a recommendation, giving reasons.

Resources
Pupil Book page 85
internet access
Data sheet: Recipes
Worksheet: Recipes

Plenary
- Ask students to compare the results and recommendations from different groups.
- Together, compile a master list of advantages and disadvantages for each recipe.

Extension work
- Ask students to write their own recipes for Yorkshire pudding, using the advantages they have identified.
- Carry out an internet search, or use Data sheet: Recipes, to compare recipes for chocolate cake.
- Ask students to report on the nutritional aspects of the recipes and choose one that seems to offer the 'healthiest option'. They should justify their choice.

Outcomes
- Students will have extracted information from tables.
- Students will have made sure the solution is presented in a clear and understandable way.

Advanced

Data sheet: Recipes

Chocolate cake recipe 1 (24 servings)	Chocolate cake recipe 2 (12 servings)
Ingredients 120 ml milk 85 g semi-sweet chocolate (grated) 300 g caster sugar 2 eggs 170 g sour cream 5 g baking powder 15 ml water 285 g sponge flour 115 g butter, softened	**Ingredients** 285 g sponge flour 5 g baking powder 3 g salt 120 ml water 84 g unsweetened chocolate 115 g butter 300 g caster sugar 2 eggs 5 ml vanilla extract 155 g sour cream
Nutrition (per serving) Total fat: 7.1 g Cholesterol: 31 mg Sodium: 92 mg Total carbohydrate: 24.4g Dietary fibre: 0.5 g Protein: 2.2 g	**Nutrition (per serving)** Total fat: 15.3 g Cholesterol: 62 mg Sodium: 299 mg Total carbohydrate: 46.3 g Dietary fibre: 1.5 g Protein: 4.2 g

 *Advanced*

Worksheet: Recipes

Checklist
- ☐ Scale recipes so they are for same number of people, for example, 12 or 1.
- ☐ Compare the cost.
- ☐ Compare the ingredients, for example, which recipe has more fat?
- ☐ Compare the guideline daily amounts for men, women and children commenting if either recipe has too much of anything bearing in mind this is only one part of one meal.
- ☐ Compare preparation times.
- ☐ Compare cooking times.
- ☐ Make a recommendation, giving reasons.

Venting gas appliances

Context

- Students are unlikely to be familiar with this unusual context, although most will live in homes with gas-powered boilers.
- Because of the very strict regulations on fitting and venting gas appliances, carbon monoxide poisoning is rare in homes.
- Some students may be aware of carbon monoxide poisoning from reading press reports and many will have detectors fitted in their homes.
- Many of the calculations involve British thermal units (Btu) and feet and inches. Students could carry out an internet search to find out the relationship between Btu and metric equivalents.

> Search the internet for 'Carbon monoxide poisoning' or 'Carbon monoxide kills' to find recent information and news stories about the dangers of CO poisoning. It may be useful to end the previous lesson with this and then distribute the Data sheet: Venting gas appliances so that students can study it before the actual lesson.

Lesson plan

Starter

- Distribute the Data sheet: Venting gas appliances at least a day before the lesson and ask students to suggest questions that could be answered from it.
- Collect these questions and ask the class, as a whole, to answer a few of them.

Main activity

- There are five tasks in this activity. The first three use information from the first page of the data sheet.
- If the data sheet was used as part of the starter activity, students will already be familiar with the information on the first page. Otherwise, go through it with the class. Explain the term **roof pitch** with reference to the diagram. It can be linked to **gradient** if this has been previously covered. Alternatively, do some work on equivalent fractions or ratio. Ask students to determine if a roof has a pitch of 5/4 what this will be in relation to the table (15/12).
- After discussion of the first page of the data sheet, students can to do tasks 1, 2 and 3. There is a worksheet for Tasks 1 and 3
- For Task 4, students will need to use information on the second page of the data sheet.
- Go through the information shown on the data sheet, referring to the diagram. Ask students why a **lateral** distance may be needed. Many of them may live in houses in which the boiler cannot vent vertically as it would need to pass through an upstairs room.

Learning objectives

Representing: recognise that a real-life problem can be solved using appropriate mathematics

Interpreting: check that a conclusion is appropriate and accurate in the context of the original problem; give a conclusion or answer to the original problem, using language and forms of presentation that make sense to a wider population

Performing: use mathematical skills and knowledge to make progress on a real-life problem, even if the situation described is not within a familiar context; give a solution to a practical problem, even if it is not within a familiar context, and make sure the solution is presented in a clear and understandable way

APP: evidence for using and applying mathematics, Shape, space and measures

PLTS: develops Creative thinkers, Team workers

Cross-curricular links: Science, ICT

© HarperCollinsPublishers 2009

 *Advanced*

- Ask some simple questions such as: 'What are the limits on the Btu output of the appliance for a height of 8 feet, a lateral of 5 feet and pipe diameter of 8 inches?' (with a fan: 83 000 Btu to 473 000 Btu; 313 000 Btu if naturally ventilated)
- Ask some reversed questions, such as: 'What combinations are possible for an appliance with a rating of 150 000 Btu per hour and venting through a pipe of diameter 5 inches?' (6 feet high pipe, lateral over 2 feet and fan assisted, 8 feet high pipe with or without a lateral and either naturally or fan ventilated)
- When students are familiar with using the table they can do Task 4.
- Task 5 is extension work and students will need to use information from both pages of the data sheet. The diagram for question 2 is available on the worksheet.

Plenary

- Discuss with students what they have learnt from doing this task.
- They are likely to have found it unusual and that looking information up in a table can be tedious. However, much mathematics when used in a practical situation is presented in tabular form as the working out of formulae has been done in advance.

Outcomes

- Students will have used scale drawing to solve a problem.
- Students will have extracted information from tables.
- Students will have used a combination of limitations to design a safe solution to a problem.

Underpinning maths:
basic numeracy
scale drawing
estimation
reading tables and drawings
ratio
gradient (optional)

Resources
Pupil Book page 87
drawing instruments
internet access
information film:
Carbon monoxide kills
(optional, from the internet)
Data sheet: Venting gas appliances
Worksheet: Venting gas appliances

Answers

Task 1

1 0   **2** 3.25 ft   **3** 18/12   **4** 2.5 feet

5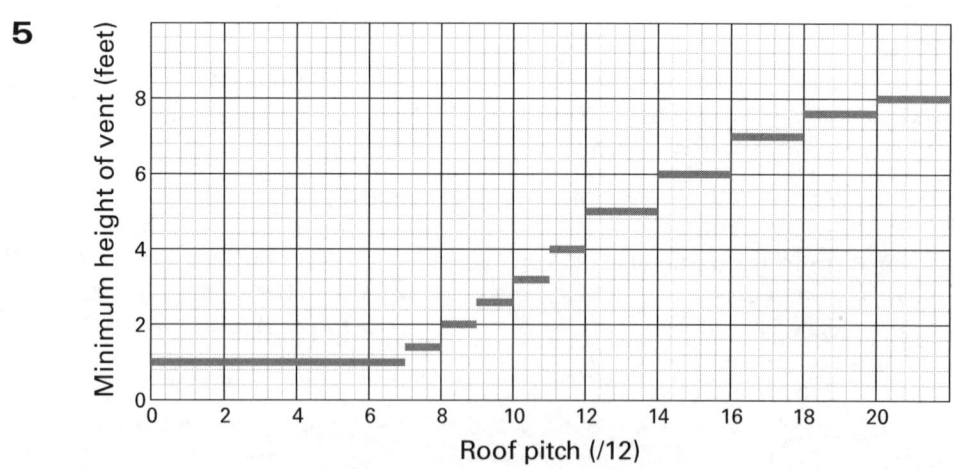

Advanced

Task 2

a No. Roof pitch is 6/12, so minimum height is 1 foot but the vent pipe is only 6 feet from the vertical wall; the minimum is 8 feet.

b Yes. Pipe is over 8 feet from the vertical wall. Roof pitch is 12/12 so the minimum pipe height is 4 feet. Pipe is just over 4 feet high.

Task 3

a Pipe at least 8 feet from vertical wall. Pitch is between 9/12 and 10/12 so the vertical height must be at least 2.5 feet.

b Pipe at least 8 feet from vertical wall. Pitch is 18/12 so the vertical height must be at least 7 feet.

Task 4

1 20 feet

2 6 inches

3 **a** 6.5 feet   **b** Yes, minimum is 2.5 feet.

4 5 feet; the minimum from the table is 10 feet but this would only extend 3.5 feet above roof. Minimum height table says 5 feet.

5 **a** 2 sq in   **b** 5 sq in   **c** 13 sq in   **d** 16 sq in

Task 5 (extension)

1 **a** H = 8 feet, L = 5 feet; fan: minimum 83 to maximum 473; natural 313

 b H = 10 feet, L = 2 feet; fan minimum 26 to maximum 289; natural 195

2 The pipe needs to be 8 feet from vertical wall so need a lateral distance of 5 feet minimum. This gives a minimum height to the roof of 9 feet. This would be OK as even an 8 foot high 6 inch pipe with 5 feet laterally has a maximum of 173 000 Btu. Pitch is 12/12, which means at least 4 feet above the roof.

© HarperCollins*Publishers* 2009

★★★ *Advanced*
Data sheet: Venting gas appliances

Roof pitch	Minimum height of vent (feet)
Flat to 7/12	1.0
Over 7/12 up to 8/12	1.5
Over 8/12 up to 9/12	2.0
Over 9/12 up to 10/12	2.5
Over 10/12 up to 11/12	3.25
Over 11/12 up to 12/12	4.0
Over 12/12 up to 14/12	5.0
Over 14/12 up to 16/12	6.0
Over 6/12 up to 18/12	7.0
Over 18/12 up to 20/12	7.5
Over 20/12 up to 21/12	8.0

Roof pitch and minimum height of vent

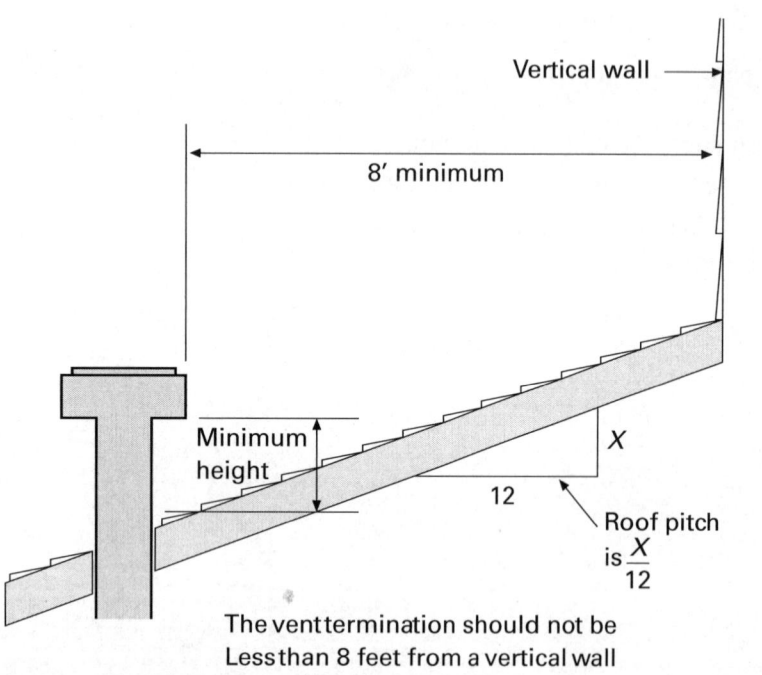

Diagram showing the position of the vent termination relative to the vertical wall

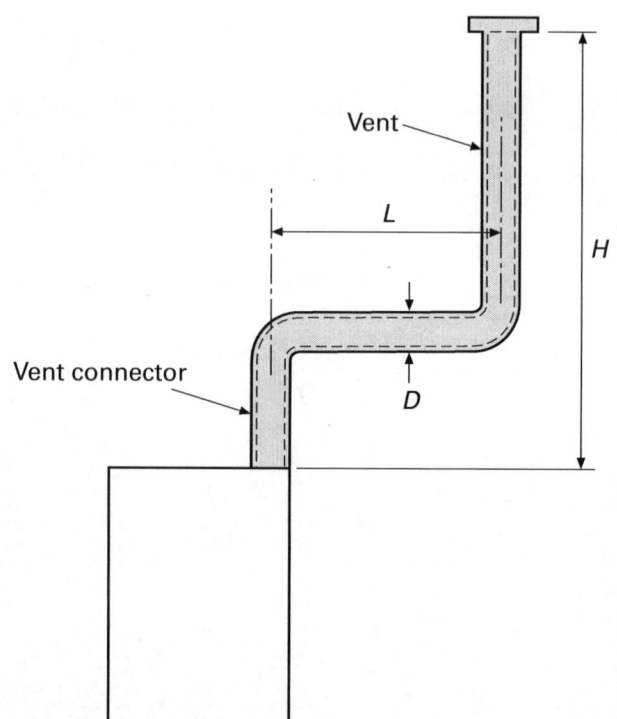

Diagram for a single gas appliance showing the diameter, D, lateral distance, L, and height, H, for vent systems

© HarperCollins*Publishers* 2009

Advanced ★★★

Vent table: capacity of Type B double-wall vents with Type B double-wall connectors serving a single category 1 appliance
FAN = fan assisted extraction. NAT = natural extraction

VENT TABLES

Capacity of Type B Double-Wall Vents with Type B Double-Wall Connectors
Serving a Single Category I Appliance

TABLE 1

Height H (ft)	Lateral L (ft)	Vent and Connector Diameter - D (inches)																			
		3"			4"			5"			6"			7"			8"			9"		
		\multicolumn{21}{c}{Appliance Input Rating in Thousands of Btu Per Hour}
		FAN		NAT	FAN		NAT	FAN		NAT	FAN		NAT	FAN		NAT	FAN		NAT	FAN		NAT
		Min	Max	Max	Min	Max	Max	Min	Max	Max	Min	Max	Max	Min	Max	Max	Min	Max	Max	Min	Max	Max
6	0	0	78	46	0	152	86	0	251	141	0	375	205	0	524	285	0	698	370	0	897	470
	2	13	51	36	18	97	67	27	157	105	32	232	157	44	321	217	53	425	285	63	543	370
	4	21	49	34	30	94	64	39	153	103	50	227	153	66	316	211	79	419	279	93	536	362
	6	25	46	32	36	91	61	47	149	100	59	223	149	78	310	205	93	413	273	110	530	354
8	0	0	84	50	0	165	94	0	276	155	0	415	235	0	583	320	0	780	415	0	1006	537
	2	12	57	40	16	109	75	25	178	120	28	263	180	42	365	247	50	483	322	60	619	418
	5	23	53	38	32	103	71	42	171	115	53	255	173	70	356	237	83	473	313	99	607	407
	8	28	49	35	39	98	66	51	164	109	64	247	165	84	347	227	99	463	303	117	596	396
10	0	0	88	53	0	175	100	0	295	166	0	447	255	0	631	345	0	847	450	0	1096	585
	2	12	61	42	17	118	81	23	194	129	26	289	195	40	402	273	48	533	355	57	684	457
	5	23	57	40	32	113	77	41	187	124	52	280	188	68	392	263	81	522	346	95	671	446
	10	30	51	36	41	104	70	54	176	115	67	267	175	88	376	245	104	504	330	122	651	427
15	0	0	94	58	0	191	112	0	327	187	0	502	285	0	716	390	0	970	525	0	1263	682
	2	11	69	48	15	136	93	20	226	150	22	339	225	38	475	316	45	633	414	53	815	544
	5	22	65	45	30	130	87	39	219	142	49	330	217	64	463	300	76	620	403	90	800	529
	10	29	59	41	40	121	82	51	206	135	64	315	208	84	445	288	99	600	386	116	777	507
	15	35	53	37	48	112	76	61	195	128	76	301	198	98	429	275	115	580	373	134	755	491
20	0	0	97	61	0	202	119	0	349	202	0	540	307	0	776	430	0	1057	575	0	1384	752
	2	10	75	51	14	149	100	18	250	166	20	377	249	33	531	346	41	711	470	50	917	612
	5	21	71	48	29	143	96	38	242	160	47	367	241	62	519	337	73	697	460	86	902	599
	10	28	64	44	38	133	89	50	229	150	62	351	228	81	499	321	95	675	443	112	877	576
	15	34	58	40	46	124	84	59	217	142	73	337	217	94	481	308	111	654	427	129	853	557
	20	48	52	35	55	116	78	69	206	134	84	322	206	107	464	295	125	634	410	145	830	537
30	0	0	100	64	0	213	128	0	374	220	0	587	336	0	853	475	0	1173	650	0	1548	855
	2	9	81	56	13	166	112	14	283	185	18	432	280	27	613	394	33	826	535	42	1072	700
	5	21	77	54	28	160	108	36	275	176	45	421	273	58	600	385	69	811	524	82	1055	688
	10	27	70	50	37	150	102	48	262	171	59	405	261	77	580	371	91	788	507	107	1028	668
	15	33	64	NR	44	141	96	57	249	163	70	389	249	90	560	357	105	765	490	124	1002	648
	20	56	58	NR	53	132	90	66	237	154	80	374	237	102	542	343	119	743	473	139	977	628
	30	NR	NR	NR	73	113	NR	88	214	NR	104	346	219	131	507	321	149	702	444	171	929	594
50	0	0	101	67	0	216	134	0	397	232	0	633	363	0	932	518	0	1297	708	0	1730	952
	2	8	86	61	11	183	122	14	320	206	15	497	314	22	715	445	26	975	615	33	1276	813
	5	20	82	NR	27	177	119	35	312	200	43	487	308	55	702	438	65	960	605	77	1259	798
	10	26	76	NR	35	168	114	45	299	190	56	471	298	73	681	426	86	935	589	101	1230	773
	15	59	70	NR	42	158	NR	54	287	180	66	455	288	85	662	413	100	911	572	117	1203	747
	20	NR	NR	NR	50	149	NR	63	275	169	76	440	278	97	642	401	113	888	556	131	1176	722
	30	NR	NR	NR	69	131	NR	84	250	NR	99	410	259	123	605	376	141	844	522	161	1125	670
100	0	NR	NR	NR	0	218	NR	0	407	NR	0	665	400	0	997	560	0	1411	770	0	1908	1040
	2	NR	NR	NR	10	194	NR	12	354	NR	13	566	375	18	831	510	21	1155	700	25	1536	935
	5	NR	NR	NR	26	189	NR	33	347	NR	40	557	369	52	820	504	60	1141	692	71	1519	926
	10	NR	NR	NR	33	182	NR	43	335	NR	53	542	361	68	801	493	80	1118	679	94	1492	910
	15	NR	NR	NR	40	174	NR	50	321	NR	62	528	353	80	782	482	93	1095	666	109	1465	895
	20	NR	NR	NR	47	166	NR	59	311	NR	71	513	344	90	763	471	105	1073	653	122	1438	880
	30	NR	NR	NR	NR	NR	NR	78	290	NR	92	483	NR	115	726	449	131	1029	627	149	1387	849
	50	NR	NR	NR	NR	NR	NR	NR	NR	NR	147	428	NR	180	651	405	197	944	575	217	1288	787

© HarperCollins*Publishers* 2009

★★★ *Advanced*
Worksheet: Venting gas appliances

Task 1
5

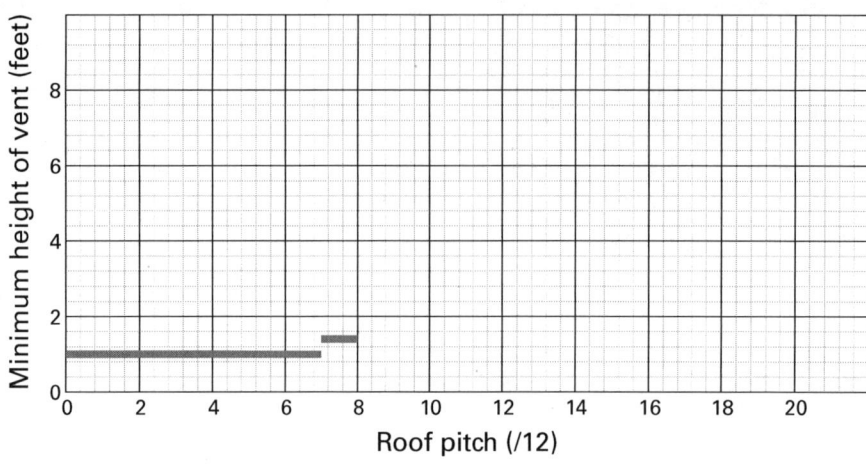

Task 3
a

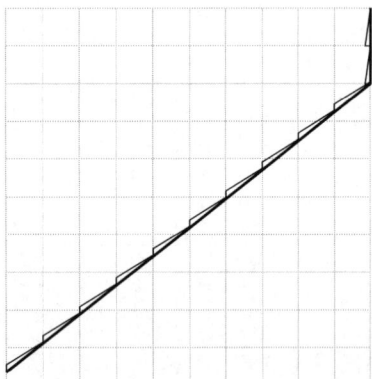

b

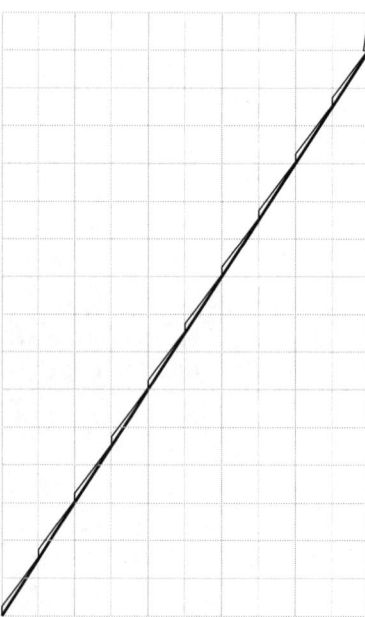

© HarperCollins*Publishers* 2009

Worksheet: Venting gas appliances

Advanced ★★★

Task 5 (extension)

2

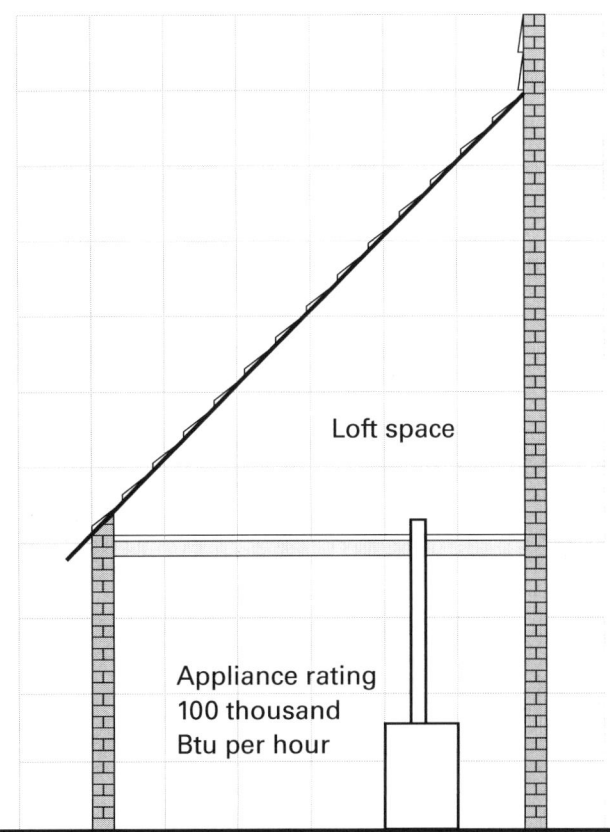

Timetables

Context
- This is an open-ended activity, in that there will be many different solutions, but it is structured since some basic rules have been laid out.
- There are a number of approaches to this task, for example, students could just choose a time and set off, or decide what time they would like to arrive and work backwards.

Lesson plan

Starter
- Show students the timetables on Data sheet: Timetables and ask several straightforward questions, such as:
  - At what time does the 0921 train from Trefforest arrive in Cardiff?
  - How long does this journey take?
- Point out that this information is given on the timetable and they do not have to do a calculation.
- Ask more questions, such as:
  - Approximately how long does it take to get by train from Cardiff to London?
  - How often do the Eurostar trains run?

Main activity
- This task is probably most successful if students work in small groups.
- Explain the task to the students, pointing out that they have to leave on a Saturday and return on a Monday.
- Make sure that students understand the restrictions placed on them. Allowing at least 15 minutes between trains at Cardiff Central means there must be 15 minutes between the arrival of the train from Trefforest and the departure of the train to London.
- Ask students why this is necessary.
- Students could allow longer than 15 minutes if they wanted to.
- Students may wish to allow time at London St Pancras to shop, before checking in at least 30 minutes before departure on Eurostar.
- Explain that this is a leisure trip. Therefore they do not have to be rigid with timings but they do need to explain any decisions they make. For example, if they decide to stay at St Pancras for 2 hours before departure they have to explain what they will be doing and at what time they will go to check in.
- Depending on the ability of the group, they could just plan the single journey to Brussels rather than the return journey.
- Students should complete a plan, either using the table or in the form of a report. There is a Worksheet for this task if required.

Learning objectives

Representing: recognise that a real-life problem can be solved using appropriate mathematics

Analysing: find a result or solution to the original problem

Performing: give a conclusion or answer to the original problem, using language and forms of presentation that make sense to a wider population

Interpreting: analyse the situation or problem and decide which is the appropriate mathematical method needed to tackle it

APP: evidence for Using and applying mathematics, Algebra

PLTS: develops Self-managers, Reflective thinkers

Cross-curricular links: ICT, French, Geography

Underpinning maths:
reading and interpreting timetables
calculating with time

© HarperCollins*Publishers* 2009

Plenary

- Ask students to present their plans and check that all the conditions have been met.

Extension work

- Students should now build in their own conditions, such as allowing time for a meal in London, missing a train connection, adding in the time to arrive at Trefforest station (a 15-minute walk) or the time from the station in Brussels to the hotel.

Outcomes

- Students will have extracted information from tables.
- Students will have had the opportunity to use basic numeracy in a real-life situation.
- Students will have used a combination of limitations to design a solution to a problem.

Advanced

Underpinning maths:
reading and interpreting timetables
calculating with time

Resources
Pupil Book page 92
internet access
Data sheet: Timetables
Worksheet: Timetables

Data sheet: Timetables

Timetable: Trefforest–Cardiff

Monday to Friday always runs — Outward

		AW	AW	AW	AW	AW	AW	AW	AW	AW	AW	AW	AW	AW	AW	AW	AW	AW
																	1	2
Trefforest	dep.	08:12	08:21	08:27	08:42	08:51	08:57	09:12	09:21	09:27	09:42	09:51	09:57	10:12	10:21	10:27	10:42	10:57	11:07	11:12	11:21	11:27	11:42	11:51
Cardiff Central	arr.	08:39	08:52	08:54	09:09	09:22	09:24	09:39	09:52	09:54	10:09	10:22	10:24	10:39	10:52	10:54	11:09	11:24	11:34	11:39	11:52	11:54	12:09	12:22
Duration		0:27	0:31	0:27	0:27	0:31	0:27	0:27	0:31	0:27	0:27	0:31	0:27	0:27	0:31	0:27	0:27	0:27	0:27	0:27	0:31	0:27	0:27	0:31
Changes		0	0	0	0	0	0	0	0	0	0	0	0	0	0	0	0	0	0	0	0	0	0	0
Seating Class		S	S	S	S	S	S	S	S	S	S	S	S	S	S	S	S	S	S	S	S	S	S	S
Catering																								

Saturday always runs — Outward

		AW	AW	AW	AW	AW	AW	AW	AW	AW	AW	AW	AW	AW	AW	AW	AW	AW
																	1	2
Trefforest	dep.	08:12	08:27	08:42	08:51	08:57	09:12	09:21	09:27	09:42	09:51	09:57	10:12	10:21	10:27	10:42	10:57	11:07	11:12	11:21	11:27	11:42	11:51
Cardiff Central	arr.	08:39	08:54	09:09	09:22	09:24	09:39	09:52	09:54	10:09	10:22	10:24	10:39	10:52	10:54	11:09	11:24	11:34	11:39	11:52	11:54	12:09	12:22
Duration		0:27	0:27	0:27	0:31	0:27	0:27	0:31	0:27	0:27	0:31	0:27	0:27	0:31	0:27	0:27	0:27	0:27	0:27	0:31	0:27	0:27	0:31
Changes		0	0	0	0	0	0	0	0	0	0	0	0	0	0	0	0	0	0	0	0	0	0
Seating Class		S	S	S	S	S	S	S	S	S	S	S	S	S	S	S	S	S	S	S	S	S	S
Catering																							

Monday to Friday always runs — Return

		AW	AW	AW	AW	AW	AW	AW	AW	AW	AW	AW	AW	AW	AW	AW	AW
														5	6		
Cardiff Central	dep.	18:06	18:11	18:26	18:36	18:41	19:06	19:11	19:26	19:41	20:06	20:26	20:41	21:06	21:26	21:41	22:06
Trefforest	arr.	18:31	18:35	18:52	19:00	19:10	19:31	19:35	19:52	20:05	20:31	20:52	21:05	21:31	21:52	22:05	22:31
Duration		0:25	0:24	0:26	0:24	0:29	0:25	0:24	0:26	0:24	0:25	0:26	0:24	0:25	0:26	0:24	0:25
Changes		0	0	0	0	0	0	0	0	0	0	0	0	0	0	0	0
Seating Class		S	S	S	S	S	S	S	S	S	S	S	S	S	S	S	S
Catering																	

Saturday always runs — Return

		AW	AW	AW	AW	AW	AW	AW	AW	AW	AW	AW	AW	AW	AW	AW	AW
														5	6		
Cardiff Central	dep.	18:06	18:11	18:26	18:36	18:41	19:06	19:11	19:26	19:41	20:06	20:26	20:41	21:06	21:26	21:41	22:06
Trefforest	arr.	18:31	18:35	18:52	19:00	19:10	19:31	19:35	19:52	20:05	20:31	20:52	21:05	21:31	21:52	22:05	22:31
Duration		0:25	0:24	0:26	0:24	0:29	0:25	0:24	0:26	0:24	0:25	0:26	0:24	0:25	0:26	0:24	0:25
Changes		0	0	0	0	0	0	0	0	0	0	0	0	0	0	0	0
Seating Class		S	S	S	S	S	S	S	S	S	S	S	S	S	S	S	S
Catering																	

© HarperCollins*Publishers* 2009

Timetable: Cardiff–London

Monday to Friday always runs
Outward

		GW	GW	GW	GW	GW	GW	GW	GW	GW
Cardiff Central	dep.	08:25	08:55	09:25	09:55	10:25	10:55	11:25	11:55	12:25
London Paddington	arr.	10:32	11:02	11:32	12:00	12:32	13:09	13:30	14:06	14:32
Duration		2:07	2:07	2:07	2:05	2:07	2:14	2:05	2:11	2:07
Changes		0	0	0	0	0	0	0	0	0
Seating Class		1st	1st	1st	1st	1st	1st	1st	1st	1st
Catering		H	H	☕	☕	☕	☕	☕	☕	H

Saturday always runs
Outward

		GW	GW	GW	GW	GW
Cardiff Central	dep.	08:25	09:25	10:25	11:25	12:25
London Paddington	arr.	10:37	11:37	12:37	13:37	14:38
Duration		2:12	2:12	2:12	2:12	2:13
Changes		0	0	0	0	0
Seating Class		1st	1st	1st	1st	1st
Catering		☕	☕	☕	☕	☕

Monday to Friday always runs
Return

		GW	GW	GW	GW	GW	GW
London Paddington	dep.	18:15	18:45	19:15	20:15	21:15	22:45
Cardiff Central	arr.	20:27	20:48	21:21	22:25	23:37	01:14
Duration		2:12	2:03	2:06	2:10	2:22	2:29
Changes		0	0	0	0	0	0
Seating Class		1st	1st	1st	1st	1st	1st
Catering		☕	☕	☕	☕	☕	☕

Saturday always runs
Return

		GW	GW	GW	GW
London Paddington	dep.	18:45	19:45	20:45	22:00
Cardiff Central	arr.	20:48	21:47	23:06	00:19
Duration		2:03	2:02	2:21	2:19
Changes		0	0	0	0
Seating Class		1st	1st	1st	1st
Catering		☕	☕	☕	☕

© HarperCollinsPublishers 2009

Advanced

Timetable: Eurostar, London–Brussels

London ▸ Paris/Brussels

Monday to Friday

Notes	LONDON	EBBSFLEET	ASHFORD	CALAIS	LILLE	BRUSSELS	PARIS	Train no
	05:25	05:42	-	-	-	-	08:50	9078
	05:57	-	06:27	-	-	08:56		9106
1	06:26	06:42	-	-	-	-	09:47	9002
	06:55	-	07:25	-	-	-	10:17	9004
	06:59	07:15	-	-	09:24	10:03		9110
	07:27	07:45	-	09:29	-	-	10:56	9006
	08:32	-	-	-	-	-	11:47	9010
	08:34	-	-	-	-	11:29		9120
	09:01	-	-	-	11:21	-	12:23	9012
	09:26	09:42	-	-	-	-	12:47	9014
	09:53	-	10:28	-	12:24			9074
	10:25	-	10:55	-	-	-	13:47	9018
	10:57	11:15	-	-	13:24	14:03		9126
1	11:32	-	-	-	-	-	14:47	9022
	12:29	12:45	-	-	-	-	15:50	9024
	12:57	13:15	-	-	15:24	16:03		9132
	13:32	-	-	-	-	-	16:47	9028
	14:04	-	-	-	16:24	-	17:26	9030
	14:34	-	-	-	16:54	17:33		9138
	15:29	15:45	-	17:29	-	-	18:56	9036
1	16:04	-	-	-	-	18:59		9144
2	16:04	-	-	-	18:24	19:03		9144
	16:25	-	16:55	-	-	-	19:47	9040
	17:27	17:45	-	-	19:54	20:33		9150
	17:30	-	-	-	-	-	20:47	9044
	17:56	18:12	-	-	-	-	21:17	9046
	18:32	-	-	-	-	-	21:47	9048
	18:35	-	-	-	-	21:33		9154
	19:02	-	-	-	-	-	22:17	9050
1	19:32	-	-	-	-	-	22:47	9052
	19:34	-	-	-	21:54	22:33		9158
	20:05	-	-	21:59	-	-	23:26	9054

Saturday and Sunday

Notes	LONDON	EBBSFLEET	ASHFORD	CALAIS	LILLE	BRUSSELS	PARIS	Train no
3	06:22	06:39	-	-	-	-	09:47	9002
3	06:55	-	07:25	-	-	-	10:17	9004
3	06:59	07:15	-	-	09:24	10:03		9110
3	07:27	07:45	-	09:29	-	-	10:56	9006
3	07:57	-	08:28	-	-	10:56		9114
4	07:52	08:09	-	-	-	-	11:17	9008
3	08:32	-	-	-	-	-	11:47	9010
3	08:59	09:15	-	-	11:24	12:03		9116
	09:26	09:42	-	-	-	-	12:47	9014
	09:53	-	10:28	-	12:24			9074
3 5	10:00	-	-	-	-	-	13:17	9016
	10:25	-	10:55	-	-	-	13:47	9018
	10:57	11:15	-	-	13:24	14:03		9126
	11:00	-	-	-	-	-	14:17	9020
4	12:02	-	-	-	-	-	15:17	9082
	12:29	12:45	-	14:29	-	-	15:56	9024
	12:57	13:15	-	-	15:24	16:03		9132
4	13:00	-	-	-	-	-	16:17	9026
3	13:32	-	-	-	-	-	16:47	9028
	14:04	-	-	-	16:24	-	17:26	9030
	14:34	-	-	-	16:54	17:33		9138
	15:29	15:45	-	17:29	-	-	18:56	9036
4	16:04	-	-	17:59	-	19:03		9144
	16:25	-	16:55	-	-	-	19:47	9040
	16:57	17:15	-	-	19:24	20:03		9148
	17:31	-	-	19:26	-	-	20:53	9044
	17:56	18:12	-	-	-	-	21:17	9046
4	18:21	-	18:55	-	20:51	21:33		9154
3	18:56	19:12	-	-	-	-	22:17	9050
4	19:02	-	-	-	-	-	22:17	9050
	19:34	-	-	-	21:54	22:33		9158
	20:05	-	-	-	-	-	23:20	9054
4	20:32	-	-	-	-	-	23:47	9056

Paris/Brussels ▸ London

Monday to Friday

Notes	PARIS	BRUSSELS	LILLE	CALAIS	ASHFORD	EBBSFLEET	LONDON	Train no
	06:43	-	-	-	-	-	07:58	9005
		06:59	07:35	-	-	-	07:55	9109
	07:13	-	-	-	-	-	08:28	9007
		08:05	-	-	-	-	08:56	9113
	07:43	-	-	-	-	-	08:59	9009
	08:07	-	-	09:34	-	09:18	09:34	9011
	09:13	-	-	-	10:06	-	10:36	9015
		09:29	10:05	-	-	10:15	10:31	9119
	10:13	-	-	-	-	-	11:28	9019
	11:13	-	-	-	-	-	12:29	9023
		11:29	12:05	-	-	-	12:26	9181
	12:13	-	-	-	-	-	13:28	9027
	13:01	-	14:04	14:34	-	14:18	14:34	9031
1	14:13	-	-	-	-	-	15:29	9035
		14:59	15:35	-	-	-	15:56	9141
	15:13	-	-	-	16:06	-	16:36	9039
		15:59	16:35	-	-	16:45	17:03	9145
	16:13	-	-	-	-	17:18	17:34	9043
		16:59	17:35	-	17:37	-	18:07	9149
	17:13	-	-	-	-	18:18	18:34	9047
1	17:43	-	-	-	-	-	18:59	9049
		17:59	18:35	-	-	18:45	19:03	9153
	18:13	-	-	-	-	19:18	19:34	9051
	18:43	-	-	-	19:36	-	20:06	9053
		18:59	19:35	-	-	-	19:56	9157
	19:13	-	-	-	-	20:18	20:34	9055
		20:38	-	20:37	-	-	21:12	9057
	20:13	-	-	-	-	-	21:29	9059
		20:29	21:05	-	-	21:15	21:33	9163
	21:13	-	-	-	-	22:18	22:34	9063

Saturday and Sunday

Notes	PARIS	BRUSSELS	LILLE	CALAIS	ASHFORD	EBBSFLEET	LONDON	Train no
3		06:59	07:35	-	-	-	07:55	9109
3	07:13	-	-	-	-	-	08:28	9007
3		07:59	-	09:02	-	-	08:56	9113
4		07:59	08:35	-	-	-	08:57	9113
	08:07	-	-	09:34	-	09:18	09:34	9011
	09:13	-	-	-	10:06	-	10:36	9015
3		09:29	10:05	-	-	10:15	10:31	9119
	10:13	-	-	-	-	-	11:28	9019
	11:13	-	-	-	-	-	12:29	9023
4	11:43	-	-	-	-	-	12:59	9025
		11:29	12:05	-	-	-	12:26	9181
	12:13	-	-	-	-	-	13:28	9027
		12:59	13:35	-	-	13:45	14:03	9133
	13:01	-	14:04	14:34	-	14:18	14:34	9031
4	13:43	-	-	-	-	-	14:59	9033
	14:13	-	-	-	-	-	15:29	9035
		14:29	15:05	-	-	-	15:26	9139
	15:07	-	-	16:34	16:06	-	16:36	9039
	16:13	-	-	-	-	17:18	17:34	9043
4		16:59	17:35	-	17:33	-	18:03	9149
	17:13	-	-	-	-	18:18	18:34	9047
4	17:43	-	-	-	-	-	18:59	9049
		17:59	18:35	-	-	18:45	19:03	9153
	18:13	-	-	-	-	19:18	19:34	9051
4		18:59	19:35	-	-	-	19:56	9157
4	19:13	-	-	-	-	-	20:29	9055
		20:38	-	20:37	-	-	21:12	9057
	20:13	-	-	-	21:06	21:24	21:41	9059
4	20:43	-	-	-	-	-	21:59	9061
4		20:29	21:05	-	-	21:15	21:33	9163
	21:13	-	-	-	-	22:18	22:34	9063

© HarperCollins*Publishers* 2009

Worksheet: Timetables

Advanced

	Time	Time taken
Depart Trefforest		–
Arrive Cardiff Central		
Depart Cardiff Central		
Arrive London Paddington		
Depart London Paddington		
Arrive London St Pancras		
Depart London St Pancras		
Arrive Brussels		
		Total time taken =

	Time	Time taken
Depart Brussels		–
Arrive London St Pancras		
Depart London St Pancras		
Arrive London Paddington		
Depart London Paddington		
Arrive Cardiff Central		
Depart Cardiff Central		
Arrive Trefforest		
		Total time taken =

© HarperCollins*Publishers* 2009

Alcohol

Context

- This context will be very familiar to students. Alcohol, binge-drinking, drink–driving and the social effects of excessive use of alcohol will have been issues discussed in other subjects and also on TV and radio.
- The activity will – hopefully – highlight some of the dangers of misuse of alcohol.

Lesson plan

Starter

- Metric and imperial units of volume are used throughout the tasks. Students would benefit from being reminded about litres, centilitres and millilitres, pints and imperial–metric conversions.
- Some body weights are given in pounds (lb). Again, students would benefit from being reminded about kilograms, grams, pounds and imperial–metric conversions.
- Any recent relevant article on alcohol use or its effects, such as a recent car crash or trouble in the local town, will be a useful starting point for a discussion.
- Ask students what they know about alcohol and its effects. For example, ask these questions.
  - How much is a unit of alcohol? (defined in the Pupil Book)
  - What is the legal drinking age? (18 as an individual buying or drinking alone in a licensed premises, but 16- and 17-year-olds may drink in a restaurant if accompanied by an adult – and it is not yet illegal for anyone over the age of 5 to drink alcohol elsewhere)
  - What is the legal limit for driving after drinking alcohol? (80 ml per litre of blood)
- Ask students if they know of any ways to lessen the effects of alcohol. They are likely to have many misconceptions such as:
  - eating a big meal
  - drinking coffee
  - sucking mints.
- There are many websites that expose the drink–driving myths. Students could find out more through an internet search.
- Bear in mind that some students may have had a recent or past tragedy in their lives caused by drink or, indeed, be living in a household with an alcoholic parent. This can be a source of embarrassment or a potential source of useful information.

Main activity

- Look at the Pupil Book with the students.
- The first graph shows the average amount of pure alcohol consumed per person over 14 years old in the last century.

Learning objectives

Representing: recognise that a real-life problem can be solved using appropriate mathematics

Analysing: use appropriate mathematical procedures

Interpreting: interpret results and solutions and make a generalisation about them

Performing: give a solution to a practical problem, even if it is not within a familiar context, and make sure the solution is presented in a clear and understandable way; draw a conclusion from working and provide a mathematical justification for this conclusion

APP: evidence for Using and applying mathematics, Calculating

PLTS: develops Independent enquiries, Effective participators

Cross-curricular links: ICT, Art and History

Underpinning maths:
percentages
metric units
imperial units
decimals
estimation

Advanced

- Ask students to interpret the graph and remark on anything it shows.
- They may be surprised to see that consumption of alcohol was very high at the turn of the last century. There are many reasons for this, which you can explore with the students. For example:
  - Drink was cheaper as it was not taxed.
  - There was one public house for approximately every 300 people.
  - There was no other entertainment and gathering in the local was better than being at home.
  - Life expectancy was much lower.
- Other points that could be raised are the sudden dip around 1914, due in part to World War 1, and also the arrival of alternative forms of entertainment such as motion pictures.
- Draw out that there has been a steady increase in alcohol consumption from 1950 and consumption is almost back to the same levels as at the turn of the last century.
- Once students are familiar with the graph they can do Task 1.
- In Task 2, students look at units of alcohol.
- Go through the Pupil Book text and discuss the ways of working out the units.
- Alcohol by volume may need to be defined. This is now printed on labels of all alcoholic drinks or displayed in lists in public houses.
- Once students are familiar with the definition and the means of calculation, they can do Task 2.
- In Task 3 students look at the permissible limits of alcohol in the blood for driving.
- Distribute Data sheet: Alcohol before the lesson so that students can use them to ask their own questions.
- Ask some straightforward questions about the tables, for example:
  - How many units can a man weighing 120 lbs consume before he reaches the limit?
  - How long does the body take to get rid of a unit of alcohol?
- When students are familiar with the tables they can do Task 3.
- Task 4 can be used as an extension or enrichment activity, or set for homework.

Plenary

- Ask students if their views on alcohol have changed through doing this activity.
  - Are they more aware of the dangers of excessive drinking?
  - Would they advise their friends about the dangers?

Outcomes

- Students will have used some simple mathematics to gain insight into a socially relevant situation.
- Students will have interpreted graphs.
- Students will have read data from tables.

Resources
Pupil Book page 94
relevant newspaper clippings
internet access
Data sheet: Alcohol

© HarperCollins*Publishers* 2009

 *Advanced*

Answers

Task 1

1 See the main lesson activity.
2 1950
3 12–13 litres
4 About 60
5 About 9.5

Task 2

1 a 15   b 40   c 1.375   d 1.6   e 2.3
2 a 54% b 37.5% c 11% d 8.3% e 1.8%
3 2.4
4 1.8
5 19.7

Task 3

1 She would have had 2.28 units, so will probably be over the limit.

2 Just about; she consumes 2.75 units, which would put her blood alcohol at under 9%, and she loses 3% during the course of the meal.

3 He consumes 8.6 units, which puts his blood alcohol at about 21%, but he loses about 4.5% during the 3 hours so his blood alcohol will be about 16.5%.

4 They each have about 3.75 units so the girls will have about 16% and the boys about 11%.

5 He consumes 5 units so he has a blood level of 12% and loses about 2% during the meal. He needs to lose another 2% so he needs to walk for 1 hour 20 minutes and even then he will be on the limit so probably should not drive.

© HarperCollins*Publishers* 2009

Data sheet: Alcohol

Advanced ★★★

MEN

Approximate Blood Alcohol Percentage

Units	Body Weight in Pounds								Effect on person
	100	120	140	160	180	200	220	240	
0	0	0	0	0	0	0	0	0	Safe Driving Limit
1	4	3	3	2	2	2	2	2	Impairment Begins
2	8	6	5	5	4	4	3	3	
3	11	9	8	7	6	6	5	5	Driving Skills Significantly Affected
4	15	12	11	9	8	8	7	6	
5	19	16	13	12	11	9	9	8	Legally Intoxicated
6	23	19	16	14	13	11	10	9	
7	26	22	19	16	15	13	12	11	
8	30	25	21	19	17	15	14	13	
9	34	28	24	21	19	17	15	14	
10	38	31	27	23	21	19	17	16	

Subtract 1% for each 40 minutes that elapses after drinking

Women

Approximate Blood Alcohol Percentage

Units	Body Weight in Pounds									Effect on person
	90	100	120	140	160	180	200	220	240	
0	0	0	0	0	0	0	0	0	0	Safe Driving Limit
1	5	5	4	3	3	3	2	2	2	Impairment Begins
2	10	9	8	7	6	5	5	4	4	Driving Skills Significantly Affected
3	15	14	11	11	9	8	7	6	6	
4	20	18	15	13	11	10	9	8	8	Legally Intoxicated
5	25	23	19	16	14	13	11	10	9	
6	30	27	23	19	17	15	14	12	11	
7	35	32	27	23	20	18	16	14	13	
8	40	36	30	26	23	20	18	17	15	
9	45	41	34	29	26	23	20	19	17	
10	51	45	38	32	28	25	23	21	19	

Subtract 1% for each 40 minutes that elapses after drinking

Garden designer

Context
- The activity is about scale drawing and making decisions in a real-life context.

Lesson plan

Starter
- Start by looking at the sketch of the garden and the list of features required.
- Ask the students to say how they could work out the length of the sloping wall. They could, for example, complete the scale drawing and then measure it.
- Ask students how they could achieve a lawn with an area of 16 m². They might suggest a square 4 m by 4 m, a rectangle 8 m by 2 m, or other shapes such as a triangle of base 8 m and height 4 m.
- Point out that the area of the lawn has to be **at least** 16 m² so they could make it bigger.

Main activity
- Ask students to tackle Task 1, which is to construct two scale drawings of the garden in the sketch. Students may wish to make more than two copies of their scale drawings in case they make any errors or have any changes of mind when completing Tasks 2 and 3.
- Ask students to complete Task 2.
- Ensure that students understand the term **radius**. Point out that their diagrams have to be accurate but that, for example, the centre of the pond does not have to coincide exactly with a line on the square grid.
- Students could make models of the shapes they wish to use on their square grid.
- They could make several models of the lawn, using different shapes.
- The trees could be represented by small circles.
- Explain to the students that some space will be left over after the design has been completed. It is important that the design looks balanced and the features are not all fitted closely together.
- When they have completed Task 2, ask students to do Task 3, in which they make an alternative garden design that also meets the customer's requirements.

Plenary
- Ask students to compare their two designs. Suggest they take the point of view that they are trying to sell one design to the homeowner as being better than the other.
- Students could also consider how the features could be changed, or what extra features could be included, to improve the garden.

Learning objectives

Representing: recognise that a real-life problem can be solved using appropriate mathematics; decide how to represent the problem to make it easier to solve using mathematics

Analysing: analyse a pattern or a relationship, using appropriate techniques

Interpreting: interpret results and solutions and make a generalisation about them; check that a conclusion is appropriate and accurate in the context of the original problem

Performing: use a range of mathematics to find solutions; check work and methods when tackling a problem and decide if a different approach may be more effective

APP: evidence for Using and applying mathematics, Shape, space and measures

PLTS: develops Independent enquirers, Self-managers

Cross-curricular links: ICT, Design and Technology

Extension work

- Ask students to design their own gardens, either based on their drawings of this garden or using their own plans drawn to scale.
- Ask students to make a list of the features and include the dimensions, working them out from their scale drawings, to ensure that they will all fit into their garden.

Outcomes

- Students will have made sure the solution is presented in a clear and understandable way.
- Students will have used mathematics to gain insight into a real-life problem.
- Students will have used a combination of limitations to design a solution to a problem.

Advanced

Underpinning maths:
scale drawing
measuring
plan views

Resources
Pupil Book page 97
centimetre-squared paper
internet access

Saving energy

Context
- This context will be familiar to all students. The effects of global warming and the increasing cost of energy are unlikely not to be issues discussed at home and in other subjects in school.
- This is a very open-ended activity, requiring each student (or group of students) to advise a family how they can save money and reduce their carbon emissions by adopting certain energy-saving measures.

Lesson plan

Starter
- An initial discussion on global warming and use of energy will be useful as an introduction but the main thrust of the activity is to start students thinking independently about the issues and to come up with their own ways of saving energy, and thus money, and reducing carbon emissions.
- The scenario is a family, Mr and Mrs Patel and their daughter, Zeenat, who live in a two-bedroom bungalow.
- In Task 1 students establish the annual carbon dioxide (CO_2) output of the Patels' heating system.
- In Task 2 students consider ways in which money can be saved and carbon emissions reduced.

Main activity
- Suggest that students work in pairs or small groups.
- Look at the Pupil Book and outline the scenario.
- Look at the diagram of the bungalow.
- Make sure students understand the scale and recall how to calculate the area of each room. They can now do Task 1.
- Once the students have established the figures for Task 1, they can move on to Task 2.
- Look at the various options for saving energy.
- Consider which ones might be the most useful and which may not be so useful. For example, they may already shower, rather than take baths.
- Also is it worth installing a wind power generator? There are other issues relating to this, such as planning permission and what the neighbours may think.
- It will come up in the discussion that the Patel's may already have some of these energy-saving measures in place.
- Tell the class that, although the Patels have no physical energy-saving measures, they do take showers and dry their clothes on the line when possible.
- Working in their groups, the class can produce a report for the Patels, outlining how much they could potentially save by adopting some of these measures.

Learning objectives

Representing: decide how to represent the problem to make it easier to solve using mathematics

Interpreting: check that a conclusion is appropriate and accurate in the context of the original problem; give a conclusion or answer to the original problem, using language and forms of presentation that make sense to a wider population

Performing: give a solution to a practical problem, even if it is not within a familiar context, and make sure the solution is presented in a clear and understandable way; draw a conclusion from working and provide a mathematical justification for this conclusion

APP: evidence for Using and applying mathematics

PLTS: develops Independent enquirers, Creative thinkers, Effective participators

Cross-curricular links: ICT, Geography, Science

© HarperCollins*Publishers* 2009

- Remind students that their report should contain reference to why each energy-saving measure is a good idea, how much it will save them each year and by how much their carbon footprint will be reduced.
- Task 3 can be used for enrichment or homework.

Plenary
- Ask each group to report briefly to the class on what they have recommended.

Outcomes
- Students will have used mathematics to gain insight into a real-life problem.

Advanced

Underpinning maths:
fractions
money calculations
estimation
area

Resources
Pupil Book page 99
internet access

Answers

Task 1

This answer is approximate and the student's answers could be different but should be about the same.

Area bedroom 1: just less than 12 m² so 2400 Btu per hour

Area bedroom 2: 8.75 m² so 2100 Btu per hour

Area study: 6.25 m² so 1800 Btu per hour

Area bathroom: about 6 m² so 1800 Btu per hour

Area dining room: 6 m² so 1800 Btu per hour

Area kitchen: 8.75 m² so 2100 Btu per hour

Area lounge: 16.5 m² so 3000 Btu per hour

Total: 15 000 Btu per hour

Heating is on for $5 \times (2 + 6.5) + 2 \times 16.5$ hours per week = 75.5 hours per week; 75.5 hours per week ≈ 3926 hours per year; $3926 \approx 15\,000 = 59\,000\,000$ Btu per year, 59 000 000 ≈ 60 million ≈ 40×60 kg CO_2 = 2.4 tonnes per year (1.5 million Btus ≈ 60 kg of CO_2 gas)

Task 2

This will vary according to each student or group.

Task 3 (extension)

There are many new cars that are both fuel-efficient and low carbon emitters. The road tax payable is now dependent on the emissions and for some cars the road tax is zero.

© HarperCollins*Publishers* 2009

Rugby numbers

Context
- Rugby Union has become more popular in recent years, particularly after England's victory in the World Cup.
- The women's game is growing quickly too.
- Most students will be familiar with the scoring system but they may be unaware that it has changed over the years.

Lesson plan

Starter
- It may be useful to find some rugby pictures on the internet to start the lesson.
- Ask one of the students to explain the scoring system and ensure that all students understand it.
- Ask students to do Task 1 in the Pupil Book. They could work in pairs if they wish.
- They should agree that the score is correct. After a few minutes, collect their suggestions of alternative ways to score 31 points.

More detailed guidance
- There will be lots of alternatives, some more likely than others. For example, it is rare to have a large number of dropped goals.
- Do not try to find all the alternatives, just establish that there are different methods.

Main activities

Session 1
- Begin Task 2 by establishing that a final score of four points is impossible. Encourage students to give a clear and concise explanation of why this is the case.
- Ask students to find the different ways in which various totals can be achieved. Again, they could work in pairs on this task.
- Encourage students to record the different ways of scoring the totals.
- Because a drop goal and a penalty goal score the same number of points, there are many variations that use the same subset. For example, 6 must be 3 + 3 but it could be 2 drop goals, 2 penalties or one of each. It is worth deciding with the students at the beginning that these will both be considered as goals. Then there is just one way of getting 6; it is 2 goals.

More detailed guidance
- A systematic approach will work best, starting from the lowest possible total and gradually increasing.
- Students will need to find an orderly way of recording the different ways of achieving the various totals. This will also help them to spot patterns in their solutions.

Learning objectives

Representing: decide which methods to use to make progress with the solution

Analysing: establish a pattern or relationship and then change the variables to see how this changes the results; test generalisations and draw conclusions from the mathematical analysis

Performing: use mathematical skills and knowledge to make progress on a problem, even if it does not use a routine mathematical procedure; analyse the situation or problem and decide which is the appropriate mathematical method needed to tackle it

APP: evidence for Using and applying mathematics, Numbers and the number system

PLTS: develops Creative thinkers, Effective participators

Cross-curricular links: ICT, PE

Rich Task

- Avoid the temptation to give students too much guidance too quickly on the best method to use. One of the objectives is for students to decide for themselves how to tackle a problem.
- Scores of 1, 2 and 4 are impossible. The first that can be made in more than one way (using the 'goals' convention mentioned above) is 10.

Underpinning maths:
recognising and extending number patterns sequences

Plenary 1
- Gather and display students' findings.
- Take suggestions about the best way to set these out.
- Ask students to describe any patterns they can see.
  - Are there any gaps?
  - Are there any general rules?

Resources
Pupil Book page 104
internet access

More detailed guidance
- Patterns that students may describe may include the following.
  - Multiples of 3 can be achieved just with goals.
  - For any particular pattern, you can go up in 5s by adding tries (7 is 1 try and 1 conversion; 12 is 2 tries and 1 conversion...).

Session 2
- Explain to students that the points awarded for a try have changed over the years and they have scored 5 only since 1992. Previously it was 4 and, before that, 3. Details are given in the Pupil Book. In Task 3, students recalculate the scores of the match in the example, using these older systems.
- Discuss briefly what difference it made. In this case, the scores were closer together but Leicester still won.
- Now move on to Task 4, in which students are asked to try to create some outcomes that would be reversed if we reverted to the pre-1971 3-point-try system.
- Let them decide for themselves about the best way to tackle this. They could continue to work in pairs.

More detailed guidance
- Here again it is important to let the students decide for themselves how to tackle the problem and to develop an efficient strategy if they can. The strategy is more important than the answer.
- If you are doing this at the right time of year you will easily be able to get some recent results to analyse and see if the outcomes would be different with a revised scoring system.

Plenary 2
- Invite students to give some specific examples and then ask if there are any general features that help in solving the problem.
- Finally, ask them to consider why the number of points for a try was increased.

More detailed guidance
- The effect of changing the number of points from 5 to 3 is to reduce the points for each try by 2. Therefore the winner is likely to change if, initially, the scores are close together but the team with more tries is the winner.
- If there are more points for a try then scoring them becomes more important and this will affect the way in which the game is played.

© HarperCollins*Publishers* 2009

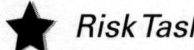 *Risk Task*

Outcomes

- Students will have had an opportunity to find and explain patterns and relationships and see the effect on answers of changing values.
- They will draw conclusions in the light of the situation and explain their reasoning.
- They will learn the importance of recording solutions in a methodical manner.
- They will have opportunities to review their findings.

Join a group

Context
- It is often useful to get people to work together in a group.
- In this activity, students look at restrictions that there might be on sizes of groups.

Lesson plan

Starter
- Ask the students to do Task 1 from the Pupil Book.
- Allow a few minutes then draw the class together and introduce Task 2.
- Ask:
  - Suppose we have 30 people in the class and we want to put them all in groups of equal size. No one should be left out. How could we do it?
- Possible answers are 15 groups of 2, 10 groups of 3 and so on.
- Note that groups of 4 are not possible if every group must be the same size.

More detailed guidance
- Task 1 is intended as a quick introduction to the ideas in this activity.
- Students will have experienced different seating arrangements in different lessons and will have varying feelings about the arrangements.
- In Task 2, students may mention factors, but do not introduce the term yourself. Part of the object of this exercise is to see if students can apply their knowledge in a new situation. It would therefore be best not to do this task if they have recently studied factors and prime numbers.
- The possible answers (excluding one large group or students working alone) are shown in this table.

Group size	2	3	5	6	10	15
Number	15	10	6	5	3	2

- Students do not need to produce the table, they can simply list the possibilities.
- Students may comment on patterns, for example,
  - You can have 5 groups of 6 or 6 groups of 5, swapping the numbers round.
  Such comments should be welcomed.

Main activities

Session 1
- Ask students to work in pairs to do Task 3 from the Pupil Book.
- Each pair should choose one of the possible group sizes.

Learning objectives

Representing: recognise that a real-life problem can be solved using appropriate mathematics

Analysing: establish a pattern or relationship and then change the variables to see how this changes the results

Interpreting: test generalisations and draw conclusions from the mathematical analysis

Performing: use mathematical skills and knowledge to make progress on a real-life problem, even if the situation described is not within a familiar context; use a range of mathematics to find solutions

APP: evidence for Using and applying mathematics, Shape, space and measures, Number and the number system

PLTS: develops Self-managers, Reflective learners

Underpinning maths:
multiples and factors
prime numbers
scale drawing

© HarperCollins Publishers 2009

 *Rich Task*

- They make a sketch of how the furniture in the classroom could be arranged to accommodate all the required groups. They should include the positions of chairs.

More detailed guidance
- Students should not take any measurements at this stage. A sketch is all that is needed. They should provide just enough detail to give an idea of where the tables and chairs will be placed.
- Make sure that all or most of the possible group sizes are covered.

Plenary 1
- Choose two or three pairs to explain their plans.
- After discussion, ask students to give the requirements of a satisfactory arrangement for a given group size.
- These could include:
  - enough room to sit down
  - enough room to walk around
  - seating around the table rather than in a line
  - everyone being able to see the board at the front.

More detailed guidance
- There is no need to take feedback from everyone, just choose a couple of pairs who were working on different group sizes.
- Ask what problems arose when students were trying to do this task. Answers could include:
  - not enough tables
  - hard to fit in all the chairs
  - not sure if it would fit.
- Discussion of problems could lead into the question:
  - *What do you need for a satisfactory arrangement for a given group size?*
- The list above is not definitive and students may well suggest other problems.
- The purpose of listing these requirements is to allow an evaluation after the next task. Save the list of requirements and make it available for display, either electronically or as a wall chart.

Session 2
- Ask students, still working in pairs, to do Task 4. They need to take measurements and make an accurate scale drawing of the room. Then they need to add the furniture, to show the arrangement they sketched earlier (or a different one if they wish to change their minds).
- Explain that, when they have completed the scale drawings, students will be asked to make an evaluation of their arrangement, using the criteria agreed earlier.
- Allow students to make their own decisions about scale and method. Only make suggestions if they are completely stuck.
- Some students may choose to cut out scale representations of the furniture, so that they can move it around. Have the necessary resources available.
- When they have completed their drawings, ask students to make their evaluations and record their findings.

Resources
Pupil Book page 106
paper of various sizes and colours
squared paper
scissors
tape measures
metre rules
glue

© HarperCollins*Publishers* 2009

Rich Task

More detailed guidance
- Make sure there is appropriate equipment available to measure the size of the room and the furniture. Alternatively, take these measurements beforehand and make them available to students in a worksheet or by other means.
- The choice of a suitable scale needs some thought. For normal classrooms a simple scale of 1 cm to represent 1 m will produce a plan that is too small. Encourage students to make their own choice but be prepared to ask supportive questions.
  - That looks a bit small.
  - What scale could we try to make it larger?
- Cutting out plans of tables from paper makes it easier for students to experiment.
- When students are satisfied with the layout, the cut-outs can be glued in place. This avoids the need to draw them on the plan. Using different coloured paper makes an effective display.
- If the plans are put on a large piece of paper the evaluations can be added in due course and the resulting posters can be displayed around the classroom.

Plenary 2
- Allow pairs to show their plans and talk through their evaluations.
- Ask the class as a whole if there is a 'best' arrangement that meets more of the features than the others.

More detailed guidance
- The emphasis is not on right or wrong answers, or judging the quality of the scale drawing.
- Stress the use of the criteria to make objective assessments about the suitability or otherwise of any particular arrangement.
- Encourage students to make positive comments: for example:
  - Sam's arrangement gives everyone a clear view of the board.
  - In that arrangement it is easy to walk around the classroom.

Session 3
- Introduce Task 5.
  - Suppose the number of students is no longer 30 but 28?
  - What possible group sizes could we have now?
  - What about for 27 students?
- Still working in pairs, students should consider different possible class sizes. In each case, they should think what different group sizes are possible. Remind them that everyone should be included.
- Ask students to make a record of their findings, in a sensible way.
- They should look for any patterns they can see in their results and write them down.

More detailed guidance
- Students are moving from scale drawing back to number patterns here.
- Students may notice the following.
  - For prime numbers no grouping is possible.
  - The number of different possible groups varies and depends on the number of factors.
- Encourage students to think about a sensible way to record their findings. They might think of ordered lists or tables.
- Encourage students to make the decision for themselves and do not direct them to a particular method.
- Students who complete this quickly can move on to the extension work below.

© HarperCollins*Publishers* 2009

 *Rich Task*

Plenary 3

- Discuss the results that students have found and any patterns they have noted.
- Encourage the use of the terms **factor**, **multiple** and **prime number**.

More detailed guidance

- Some of results that may be found are shown in this table.

Number of students	Possible groups
27	9 groups of 3; 3 groups of 9
28	14 pairs, 7 groups of 4, 4 of 7, 2 of 14
29	None. It is a prime number
31	None. It is a prime number
32	16 pairs, 8 of 4, 4 of 8, 2 of 16
33	3 groups of 11, 11 groups of 3

- Ask questions to test students' understanding.
  - Tell me a class size where no groups are possible.
  - Tell me a class size where groups of 3 are possible.

Extension work

- If students are confident about Task 5, set them to do Task 6, in which they are asked to suppose that two classes work together in the hall, so that there are about 60 students; perhaps a few more, perhaps a few less.
- Students explore the different ways in which they could split them into groups.

More detailed guidance

- Students are expected to choose their own class sizes. Look for numbers around 60.
- The prime numbers between 50 and 70 are 53, 59, 61 and 67. These cannot have groups without remainders.
- 60 can have groups of size 2, 3, 4, 5, 6, 10, 12, 15, 20 and 30.
- Ask students why there are 60 seconds in a minute and 60 minutes in an hour. It could be because 60 has lots of factors.

Outcomes

- Students will practise evaluating an outcome using agreed criteria.
- Students will see a practical situation where factors and prime numbers are involved.

Follow that car

Context
- The registration letters on a car show where it was first registered.
- Do cars tend to stay where they were registered or do they move around the country?

Lesson plan
This activity will last for about two lessons.

Preliminary task
- A day or two before starting this activity, ask the students to complete Task 1 in the Pupil Book.
- Each student will need a copy of the Data sheet: Follow that car – information on vehicle number plates
- The task for students is to find out as much as they can from the number plate of a car with which they are familiar. This car must have a new-style number plate issued after September 2001.

More detailed guidance
- If the students are given the data sheet in advance they will be familiar with its content when they come to the first lesson.
- Before September 2001 a different system was in operation. The age of the car is revealed by the single letter (at least as far back as 1962) but all the registration district codes were different.
- Depending on the ability of the students, you may wish to explain the various parts of the data sheet when you give it out.
- Students working at level 2 should be able to tackle it without guidance.

Starter
- Ask students to do Task 2 to ensure that they understand all the information encoded in a car registration (date and area of registration). They should swap the questions that they have made up with those of a partner, answer each other's questions and then then check that they have been answered correctly.
- Allow a few minutes for students to complete this. Then ask where they think local cars are likely to have been registered. Ask what factors could affect this. Give students a short time to discuss this and then collect suggestions. Do not comment on their validity.
- Possible comments could be:
  - New cars are more likely to be registered locally.
  - Cars move round the country when they are sold.
  - Some cars are foreign imports.
  - Company cars might be different.
  - Uncommon makes might come from further away.

Learning objectives

Representing: decide which methods to use to make progress with the solution

Analysing: use appropriate mathematical procedures

Interpreting: interpret results and solutions and make a generalisation about them

Performing: draw a conclusion from working and provide a mathematical justification for this conclusion

APP: evidence for Using and applying mathematics, Handling data

PLTS: develops Independent enquirers, Team workers

Cross-curricular links: ICT

Underpinning maths:
extracting information from a variety of sources
collecting data through a survey
choosing the most appropriate way to present data

 *Rich Task*

Resources
Pupil Book page 108
stationery and equipment to display or present findings
access to ICT
internet access
Data sheet: Follow that car

More detailed guidance
- The students will find it more interesting to compose their own questions than simply answering a set of closed questions.
- If any students come up with interesting questions, share them with the rest of the class.
- The suggestions about the factors influencing the origin of cars will lead in to the next task. It does not matter what they are; the intention will be for the students to choose an aspect of car registration plates that is interesting to them and this preliminary discussion will help them to think about the possibilities. Allow time for this and do not cut the discussion short.

Main activities
Session 1
- Students should work in groups of about four as they carry out Task 3 in the Pupil Book.
- The comments from the starter might give some ideas about what they could report on. They should decide on a hypothesis they want to test or a question they wish to answer. Then they need to plan how to collect the necessary data and how they will report back the results of their survey.
- Allow time for discussion, either as a whole class or in groups, to come up with a list of things to consider. It could include:
  - an initial hypothesis or question
  - where to find the cars (school car park, students' home streets, students' family cars,…)
  - the number of cars
  - what to record (letters, age, make,…)
  - how to record it
  - how to analyse the data
  - how to display the results (graphs, tables, charts, ICT,…).
- After the discussion students should write a brief outline of their plan, covering the points raised.

More detailed guidance
- The hypothesis or question could be a simple one such as:
  - *The majority of cars are registered locally*

  or something more complex that includes more that one factor, such as:
  - *Are larger cars more likely to come from farther away?*

  Encourage students to choose something more demanding if you think they will be able to succeed with it.
- Students will have done surveys before. For this activity it is important for them to think beforehand about the purpose of the survey and how to collect suitable data. They should also consider how they intend to display the results they collect.

© HarperCollins*Publishers* 2009

Rich Task

Plenary
- Ask one or two groups to outline the task they have set themselves and what they will do to carry it out.
- As a result of the plenary discussion they may wish to make adjustments to their plans.

More detailed guidance
- Choose one or two groups with good plans to feed back to the rest of the class.
- Other groups may then wish to improve their plans in the light of what they hear.
- Allow enough time for them to do this.

Session 2: Carrying out the survey
- Students should now do Task 4, carrying out the survey they have planned.
- It will probably be convenient for students to collect the data they need as a homework assignment so that they can do the analysis in class.
- The outcome should be a poster that includes the initial hypothesis or question, charts or diagrams to display the results and the final conclusion with supporting evidence.

More detailed guidance
- Make sure that students are clear about the outcome that is expected before they start.
  - How will they be presenting their results?
- If possible, give students access to ICT resources so that they can use them for producing charts, diagrams or written reports.

Extension work
- The survey has focused on cars with new-style number plates. Students could be asked to find out about the systems that were used before the current one was introduced.

> A date letter was first introduced in 1963, as shown on the resource sheet. For a number plate such as L123 ABC the letters AB indicate the registration district. These districts were all changed in 2001. Details can be found on the internet.

Outcomes
- Students will plan and execute a survey to investigate a hypothesis chosen by them.
- Students will present their conclusions to the rest of the class.

Rich Task
Data sheet: Follow that car

Vehicle registration data

Vehicle Number Plates

For more information go to: **www.direct.gov.uk/motoring**

INF104

New Style Number Plates

A new number plate format was introduced on 1 September 2001.

At the same time new regulations took effect governing design, manufacture and display of number plates. The regulations introduce a standard typeface, making it easier for number plates to be read. The change applies to the plates of vehicles registered from 1 September 2001 and to all replacement plates issued from that date. The regulations **end** the use of italic, multiple stroke and other difficult to read lettering on number plates.

The Mandatory Typeface

An example of the new character typeface is shown below.

123456789
ABCDEFGH
JKLMNOPQ
RSTUVWXYZ

N.B: I and Q are not used in the new format. Q appears on some old format number plates, these "Q marks" will continue to be issued. See booklet INF46 "Registration numbers and you" for information.

Z is only used in the random element of the new format.

The Euro Plate

There is also provision, on a voluntary basis, for the display of the Euro symbol and GB national identifier on the plate. This enables motorists to dispense with a separate GB sticker when travelling within the EU, if they wish.

A New Format

A new registration mark system began on 1 September 2001 for all new vehicles being registered. The new format is as follows:

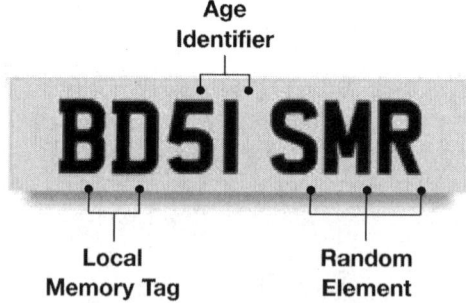

The new format will comprise seven characters and include local and age identifiers, as shown above. The local memory tag is linked to the DVLA local office where the vehicle was first registered and is intended to help witnesses recall details of the number plate.

The age identifier changes every six months in March and September. In the example above BD signifies Birmingham, 51 represents September 2001 and SMR is the random element. Lists of local memory tags and age identifiers are shown overleaf. Please note, DVLA local office identifiers may on occasion be subject to change.

Personalised Registrations

DVLA Personalised Registrations gives motorists the opportunity to purchase both prefix and current style registrations. To check the availability and price of all DVLA's Personalised Registrations visit **www.dvlaregistrations.co.uk**.

7/06

An executive agency of the Department for
Transport

Rich Task

Local Memory Tags

Letter		Local Office	DVLA local office Identifier
A	Anglia	Peterborough Norwich Ipswich	AA AB AC AD AE AF AG AH AJ AK AL AM AN AO AP AR AS AT AU AV AW AX AY
B	Birmingham	Birmingham	BA – BY
C	Cymru	Cardiff Swansea Bangor	CA CB CC CD CE CF CG CH CJ CK CL CM CN CO CP CR CS CT CU CV CW CX CY
D	Deeside to Shrewsbury	Chester Shrewsbury	DA DB DC DD DE DF DG DH DJ DK DL DM DN DO DP DR DS DT DU DV DW DX DY
E	Essex	Chelmsford	EA – EY
F	Forest & Fens	Nottingham Lincoln	FA FB FC FD FE FF FG FH FJ FK FL FM FN FP FR FS FT FV FW FX FY
G	Garden of England	Maidstone Brighton	GA GB GC GD GE GF GG GH GJ GK GL GM GN GO GP GR GS GT GU GV GW GX GY
H	Hampshire & Dorset	Bournemouth Portsmouth	HA HB HC HD HE HF HG HH HJ HK HL HM HN HO HP HR HS HT HU HV HW HX HY (HW will be used exclusively for Isle of Wight residents)
K		Luton Northampton	KA KB KC KD KE KF KG KH KJ KK KL KM KN KO KP KR KS KT KU KV KW KX KY
L	London	Wimbledon Stanmore Sidcup	LA LB LC LD LE LF LG LH LJ LK LL LM LN LO LP LR LS LT LU LV LW LX LY
M	Manchester & Merseyside	Manchester	MA – MY (MN + MAN Reserved for the Isle of Man)
N	North	Newcastle Stockton	NA NB NC ND NE NG NH NJ NK NL NM NN NO NP NR NS NT NU NV NW NX NY
O	Oxford	Oxford	OA – OY
P	Preston	Preston Carlisle	PA PB PC PD PE PF PG PH PJ PK PL PM PN PO PP PR PS PT PU PV PW PX PY
R	Reading	Reading	RA – RY
S	Scotland	Glasgow Edinburgh Dundee Aberdeen Inverness	SA SB SC SD SE SF SG SH SJ SK SL SM SN SO SP SR SS ST SU SV SW SX SY
V	Severn Valley	Worcester	VA – VY
W	West of England	Exeter Truro Bristol	WA WB WC WD WE WF WG WH WJ WK WL WM WN WO WP WR WS WT WU WV WW WX WY
Y	Yorkshire	Leeds Sheffield Beverley	YA YB YC YD YE YF YG YH YJ YK YL YM YN YO YP YR YS YT YU YV YW YX YY

N.B: DVLA cannot guarantee that any specific local memory tag or DVLA local office Identifier will be issued.

Age Identifiers

Date	Code	Date	Code
		Sept 2001 – Feb 2002	51
March 2002 – Aug 2002	02	Sept 2002 – Feb 2003	52
March 2003 – Aug 2003	03	Sept 2003 – Feb 2004	53
March 2004 – Aug 2004	04	Sept 2004 – Feb 2005	54
March 2005 – Aug 2005	05	Sept 2005 – Feb 2006	55
March 2006 – Aug 2006	06	Sept 2006 – Feb 2007	56
March 2007 – Aug 2007	07	Sept 2007 – Feb 2008	57
March 2008 – Aug 2008	08	Sept 2008 – Feb 2009	58
March 2009 – Aug 2009	09	Sept 2009 – Feb 2010	59
March 2010 – Aug 2010	10	Sept 2010 – Feb 2011	60
March 2011 – Aug 2011	11	Sept 2011 – Feb 2012	61

This pattern will continue until all permutations are exhausted.

Further information about number plates can be found on the website www.direct.gov.uk/motoring

Or you can contact Customer Enquiries (Vehicles) on 0870 240 0010 between 8.00am and 8.30pm Monday to Friday and 8.00am to 5.30pm on Saturday.

Some calls will be monitored for quality and training purposes.

Customers with impaired hearing who have a textphone/minicom should phone 01792 766426 for vehicle enquiries. You should be aware that the minicom numbers will **not** respond to ordinary telephones.

Fax: 0870 850 1285

E-mail: vehicles.dvla@gtnet.gov.uk

 *Rich Task*

Year indicators for car number plates issued from 1963 to 2001

Suffix series 1963–82 (letters)

Letter	Dates of issue
A	January 1963–December 1963
B	January 1964–December 1964
C	January 1965–December 1965
D	January 1966–December 1966
E	January 1967–July 1967
F	August 1967–July 1968
G	August 1968–July 1969
H	August 1969–July 1970
J	August 1970–July 1971
K	August 1971–July 1972
L	August 1972–July 1973
M	August 1973–July 1974
N	August 1974–July 1975
P	August 1975–July 1976
R	August 1976–July 1977
S	August 1977–July 1978
T	August 1978–July 1979
V	August 1979–July 1980
W	August 1980–July 1981
X	August 1981–July 1982
Y	August 1982–July 1983

Prefix series 1983–2001 (letters)

Letter	Dates of issue
A	August 1983–July 1984
B	August 1984–July 1985
C	August 1985–July 1986
D	August 1986–July 1987
E	August 1987–July 1988
F	August 1988–July 1989
G	August 1989–July 1990
H	August 1990–July 1991
J	August 1991–July 1992
K	August 1992–July 1993
L	August 1993–July 1994
M	August 1994–July 1995
N	August 1995–July 1996
P	August 1996–July 1997
R	August 1997–July 1998
S	August 1998–February 1999
T	March 1999–August 1999
V	September 1999–February 2000
W	March 2000–August 2000
X	September 2000–February 2001
Y	March 2001–August 2001

© HarperCollins*Publishers* 2009

Bike race

Context
- Students may be familiar bicycle track events. Team GB Cycling has been very successful in recent Olympics and World Championships. This unit looks in detail at one particular track event, the one-kilometre individual time trial, in the 2009 world cycling championships.

Lesson plan
The activity will probably last two or three lessons.

Starter
- Explain to students that they will be looking at one particular track cycling race, the individual one-kilometre time trial for men. Riders go one at a time, against the clock.
- Ask students what they think the winning time might be.
- Ask students to work in pairs for Task 1. Distribute the Data sheet: Bike race, which shows the results of the 2009 world championships. Ask students to look at the information and then write down five facts about the race.
- Allow about 5 minutes for this before asking selected students to give you facts that they have recorded.

More detailed guidance
- The winning time is usually about a minute.
- If the students generally use them, it would be appropriate to use mini-whiteboards to record the facts.
- The students might ask about the women's race; this is 500 metres, rather than 1 kilometre.
- As well as asking students for the facts recorded on the sheet, you could ask specific questions to ensure students understand the data.
  - Who won? (Rank 1 at 1000 m)
  - What was the winning time? (1.00.666)
  - What position was the British rider in? (7)
  - How many laps did they ride? (4)
  - How long was each lap? (250 m)
  - Who was in the lead at the half-way stage?
  - Approximately, what was the winner's average speed? (about 60 kph, about 37 mph)
  - Why are the times for the first lap slower than the rest? (standing start)

Learning objectives

Representing: decide how to represent the problem to make it easier to solve using mathematics

Analysing: use appropriate mathematical procedures

Interpreting: give a conclusion or answer to the original problem, using language and forms of presentation that make sense to a wider population

Performing: use mathematical skills and knowledge to make progress on a real-life problem, even if the situation described is not within a familiar context; analyse the situation or problem and decide which is the appropriate mathematical method needed to tackle it

APP: evidence for Using and applying mathematics, Calculating

PLTS: develops Independent enquirers, Effective participators

Cross-curricular links: ICT, Geography, PE

© HarperCollins Publishers 2009

 *Rich Task*

Main activities

Session 1

- Introduce Task 2. Suggest that the students work in pairs. Ask them to look at the details of the medal winners (the men who finished in the top three positions). They should notice how their race positions vary as the race progresses and that their relative order varies too.
- The times are very similar, with only about one second between first and third at the end.
- The students are asked to produce charts or graphs to show how race positions and times vary for the first three as the race progresses.
- Discuss what sort of graph would be appropriate for each set of information.
- Line graphs are probably the most appropriate. If other sorts, such as bar charts, are suggested, encourage the class to criticise and evaluate these as a choice.
- The students should also produce a brief written summary of the main points that the graphs show.

More detailed guidance

- It would be useful for students to have access to a spreadsheet when carrying out this task, although it can be done without.
- If they decide to draw a line graph of position against distance, students might think of reversing the normal order on the vertical or y-axis and putting 1 at the top.
- A graph of time against distance will not show much; the times are so close together that the lines may be indistinguishable. Lap times are not much better. One solution is to plot the differences between two riders' times. This gives graphs showing interesting variation.
- Encourage students to try out different graphs and evaluate them, by asking questions.
  - Does this show differences clearly?
  - Could I do something better?
- Avoid the temptation to tell students the best thing to do. Encourage them to try out different ideas and decide for themselves. This will be easier if they are using ICT.
- Students' comments are important. They need practice in interpreting graphs as well as drawing them.
- Students will probably like the opportunity to display their charts and comments on a poster.

Plenary 1

- Ask pairs to show and explain their charts to the class and read out their summaries.
- Students should be asked to comment on the good features of each graph.

Underpinning maths:
working with decimals to 3 decimal places
interpreting data presented in tables
selecting appropriate forms of presentation
speed

Resources
Pupil Book page 110
mini-whiteboards
computers and spreadsheet programs
internet access
Data sheet:
Bike race

© HarperCollins*Publishers* 2009

Rich Task ★★

More detailed guidance
- Encourage positive comments rather than negative ones.
  - That graph has included labels on the axes and a title.
  - That chart is large enough to read easily.
- If different pairs draw different types of charts there will be an opportunity to identify the good features of each one. This emphasises the fact that there will be a range of possible alternatives and not one right answer.

Session 2

- Look at Task 3, in which students are asked to think about the riders' times for each 125 metres of the race. Start by asking students to think about how these might vary (without doing any calculations at this stage). You could ask students, working in pairs, to look at different riders.
- Students could plot their lap times on a chart to show how they vary. Students should know by now that a line graph is the most appropriate choice.

More detailed guidance
- The riders are travelling at their slowest for the first 125 m because they have to start from rest.
- The lap times (250 metre splits) show that the riders gradually ride more slowly as the race progresses. It is likely that the 125 m times will follow a similar pattern but there might be variations.

Plenary 2

- Compare the times and charts for the different riders.
  - What are the similarities?
  - What are the differences?
  - In particular, are there differences between riders who came high in the final results and riders who came lower down?
  - Are there any particular features that make you a champion?

More detailed guidance
- None of the medallists were in a medal winning position after the first 500 metres, half-way through the race.
- Everyone went more slowly in the second half but presumably the medallists went less slowly than the others. From the results the students obtain it might be possible to put some figures to this.
- It is not important that the students reach a firm conclusion and, in any case, that may not be possible. The students are being encouraged to look at data intelligently and to try to answer the questions that it raises.

Session 3

- In Task 4 students are asked to think about the speed of the riders.
- We do not know the exact speed at any time because we do not have any speedometer readings. However, we can work out the average speed for each 125 metres by using the formula:

$$\text{average speed} = \frac{\text{distance}}{\text{time}}$$

- Students could also find the average speed for the whole race.
- Again you could ask different pairs to analyse different riders.
- Can students use the average lap times to estimate the fastest speed achieved during the race?

© HarperCollins*Publishers* 2009

 *Rich Task*

More detailed guidance

- Emphasise the difference between speed at an instant, which is the speedometer reading at a particular moment, and average speed over a particular time.
- A graph could be helpful. Ask students where they should plot the points. At 125, 250, … or in the middle of the interval, at 62.5, 187.5, …? This is similar to the issue that arises when students plot a frequency polygon from grouped data.
- Students will be finding speeds in metres per second (m/s or m s^{-1}). They may want to know what they are in mph. If so tell them that 1 m/s = 2.24 mph.

Plenary 3

- Look briefly at the estimates of the highest speeds.
- Discuss the difference between the fastest and the slowest riders.

Outcomes

- Students should be able to start from the results sheet and extract the information required to tackle the problems set.
- They should think about the most appropriate chart or graph to use and refine their choice on the basis of discussion with others and consideration of the required outcome.
- They will be able to describe what a chart shows.
- They should be able to calculate accurately using decimals to three places.
- They will have the opportunity to make calculations involving speed.
- They should make appropriate use of ICT.

© HarperCollins*Publishers* 2009

Data sheet: Bike race

Rich Task

Men's 1Km Time Trial / 1Km Contre la montre hommes
Final / Finale
Analysis / Analyse
Fri 27 Mar 2009

No 277 - ZHURKIN Nikolay (RUS)

Distance	Time	Rank	Lap Time
125m	12.187	25	
250m	19.721	26	19.721
375m	26.903	26	
500m	34.052	24	14.331
625m	41.408	25	
750m	48.982	25	14.930
875m	56.691	24	
1000m	1:04.494	24	15.512

No 306 - TSYUPYK Yuriy (UKR)

Distance	Time	Rank	Lap Time
125m	12.138	24	
250m	19.581	24	19.581
375m	26.785	25	
500m	34.111	27	14.530
625m	41.707	27	
750m	49.550	27	15.439
875m	57.694	27	
1000m	1:06.206	27	16.656

No 22 - SELZER Clemens (AUT)

Distance	Time	Rank	Lap Time
125m	11.573	9	
250m	18.697	11	18.697
375m	25.730	13	
500m	32.967	16	14.270
625m	40.390	22	
750m	48.028	22	15.061
875m	55.912	21	
1000m	1:04.077	20	16.049

No 296 - KELLAR Azikiwe (TRI)

Distance	Time	Rank	Lap Time
125m	12.433	27	
250m	19.920	28	19.920
375m	27.273	28	
500m	34.794	28	14.874
625m	42.642	28	
750m	50.919	28	16.125
875m	59.714	28	
1000m	1:08.981	28	18.062

No 196 - NITTA Yudai (JPN)

Distance	Time	Rank	Lap Time
125m	11.437	6	
250m	18.620	7	18.620
375m	25.737	14	
500m	32.960	15	14.340
625m	40.387	21	
750m	48.002	21	15.042
875m	55.739	18	
1000m	1:03.655	18	15.653

No 105 - PERALTA GASCON Juan (ESP)

Distance	Time	Rank	Lap Time
125m	12.083	23	
250m	19.485	23	19.485
375m	26.710	24	
500m	34.072	26	14.587
625m	41.650	26	
750m	49.478	26	15.406
875m	57.519	26	
1000m	1:05.823	26	16.345

No 256 - TEKLINSKI Adrian (POL)

Distance	Time	Rank	Lap Time
125m	11.593	11	
250m	18.865	14	18.865
375m	25.905	16	
500m	32.988	18	14.123
625m	40.299	19	
750m	47.878	18	14.890
875m	55.745	19	
1000m	1:03.887	19	16.009

No 81 - DITZEL Filip (CZE)

Distance	Time	Rank	Lap Time
125m	12.006	21	
250m	19.252	22	19.252
375m	26.147	21	
500m	33.127	21	13.875
625m	40.362	20	
750m	47.977	20	14.850
875m	55.988	22	
1000m	1:04.319	22	16.342

© HarperCollins*Publishers* 2009

 *Rich Task*

Men's 1Km Time Trial / 1Km Contre la montre hommes
Final / Finale
Analysis / Analyse
Fri 27 Mar 2009

No 222 - SCHMIDT Yondi (NED)			
Distance	Time	Rank	Lap Time
125m	11.311	2	
250m	18.442	5	18.442
375m	25.373	7	
500m	32.396	8	13.954
625m	39.688	9	
750m	47.238	12	14.842
875m	55.159	15	
1000m	1:03.480	17	16.242

No 262 - CHAID Gadi (RSA)			
Distance	Time	Rank	Lap Time
125m	12.501	28	
250m	19.901	27	19.901
375m	26.970	27	
500m	34.064	25	14.163
625m	41.297	24	
750m	48.841	24	14.777
875m	56.724	25	
1000m	1:04.942	25	16.101

No 78 - BABEK Tomas (CZE)			
Distance	Time	Rank	Lap Time
125m	12.064	22	
250m	19.245	21	19.245
375m	26.120	20	
500m	33.074	20	13.829
625m	40.297	18	
750m	47.886	19	14.812
875m	55.888	20	
1000m	1:04.281	21	16.395

No 161 - SEIDENBECHER Michael (GER)			
Distance	Time	Rank	Lap Time
125m	11.504	8	
250m	18.660	10	18.660
375m	25.615	10	
500m	32.632	12	13.972
625m	39.892	12	
750m	47.433	16	14.801
875m	55.306	16	
1000m	1:03.479	16	16.046

No 51 - ZHANG Miao (CHN)			
Distance	Time	Rank	Lap Time
125m	11.575	10	
250m	18.649	9	18.649
375m	25.535	9	
500m	32.588	11	13.939
625m	39.906	13	
750m	47.499	17	14.911
875m	55.362	17	
1000m	1:03.427	15	15.928

No 95 - ALONSO CASTILLO David (ESP)			
Distance	Time	Rank	Lap Time
125m	11.884	20	
250m	19.220	20	19.220
375m	26.312	22	
500m	33.422	23	14.202
625m	40.738	23	
750m	48.308	23	14.886
875m	56.193	23	
1000m	1:04.398	23	16.090

No 158 - NIMKE Stefan (GER)			
Distance	Time	Rank	Lap Time
125m	11.824	18	
250m	18.744	12	18.744
375m	25.388	8	
500m	32.068	6	13.324
625m	38.863	2	
750m	45.852	1	13.784
875m	53.105	1	
1000m	1:00.666	1	14.814

No 315 - PHINNEY Taylor (USA)			
Distance	Time	Rank	Lap Time
125m	12.227	26	
250m	19.611	25	19.611
375m	26.547	23	
500m	33.361	22	13.750
625m	40.179	17	
750m	47.124	10	13.763
875m	54.272	8	
1000m	1:01.611	2	14.487

© HarperCollins*Publishers* 2009

Rich Task ★★

Men's 1Km Time Trial / 1Km Contre la montre hommes
Final / Finale
Analysis / Analyse
Fri 27 Mar 2009

No 121 - LAFARGUE Quentin (FRA)

Distance	Time	Rank	Lap Time
125m	11.800	15	
250m	19.064	17	19.064
375m	26.024	18	
500m	32.968	17	13.904
625m	40.029	15	
750m	47.310	14	14.342
875m	54.846	12	
1000m	1:02.669	9	15.359

No 249 - KUCZYNSKI Kamil (POL)

Distance	Time	Rank	Lap Time
125m	11.444	7	
250m	18.453	6	18.453
375m	25.184	5	
500m	31.994	4	13.541
625m	39.071	5	
750m	46.439	5	14.445
875m	54.199	7	
1000m	1:02.356	8	15.917

No 225 - VELDT Tim (NED)

Distance	Time	Rank	Lap Time
125m	11.808	16	
250m	19.089	18	19.089
375m	26.052	19	
500m	32.995	19	13.906
625m	40.099	16	
750m	47.410	15	14.415
875m	55.009	13	
1000m	1:02.886	12	15.476

No 46 - LI Wen Hao (CHN)

Distance	Time	Rank	Lap Time
125m	11.809	17	
250m	18.897	15	18.897
375m	25.674	12	
500m	32.567	10	13.670
625m	39.727	10	
750m	47.217	11	14.650
875m	55.075	14	
1000m	1:03.287	14	16.070

No 133 - DANIELL David (GBR)

Distance	Time	Rank	Lap Time
125m	11.414	5	
250m	18.292	2	18.292
375m	24.906	1	
500m	31.631	1	13.339
625m	38.656	1	
750m	46.092	2	14.461
875m	54.004	3	
1000m	1:02.316	7	16.224

No 233 - DAWKINS Edward (NZL)

Distance	Time	Rank	Lap Time
125m	11.856	19	
250m	19.120	19	19.120
375m	26.003	17	
500m	32.890	14	13.770
625m	39.971	14	
750m	47.270	13	14.380
875m	54.830	10	
1000m	1:02.685	10	15.415

No 12 - SUNDERLAND Scott (AUS)

Distance	Time	Rank	Lap Time
125m	11.413	4	
250m	18.341	3	18.341
375m	25.100	3	
500m	32.022	5	13.681
625m	39.161	6	
750m	46.535	7	14.513
875m	54.176	6	
1000m	1:02.144	5	15.609

No 298 - BOLIBRUKH Yevhen (UKR)

Distance	Time	Rank	Lap Time
125m	11.680	13	
250m	18.899	16	18.899
375m	25.755	15	
500m	32.656	13	13.757
625m	39.741	11	
750m	47.123	9	14.467
875m	54.830	10	
1000m	1:02.860	11	15.737

© HarperCollins*Publishers* 2009

 *Rich Task*

Men's 1Km Time Trial / 1Km Contre la montre hommes
Final / Finale
Analysis / Analyse
Fri 27 Mar 2009

No 216 - TISIN Mohd Rizal (MAS)

Distance	Time	Rank	Lap Time
125m	11.725	14	
250m	18.826	13	18.826
375m	25.617	11	
500m	32.402	9	13.576
625m	39.319	7	
750m	46.477	6	14.075
875m	53.924	2	
1000m	1:01.658	3	15.181

No 123 - PERVIS François (FRA)

Distance	Time	Rank	Lap Time
125m	11.631	12	
250m	18.620	7	18.620
375m	25.361	6	
500m	32.230	7	13.610
625m	39.373	8	
750m	46.847	8	14.617
875m	54.688	9	
1000m	1:02.976	13	16.129

No 115 - D'ALMEIDA Michaël (FRA)

Distance	Time	Rank	Lap Time
125m	11.365	3	
250m	18.371	4	18.371
375m	25.119	4	
500m	31.945	3	13.574
625m	38.985	4	
750m	46.328	3	14.383
875m	54.004	3	
1000m	1:02.034	4	15.706

No 220 - MULDER Teun (NED)

Distance	Time	Rank	Lap Time
125m	11.171	1	
250m	18.231	1	18.231
375m	25.043	2	
500m	31.922	2	13.691
625m	38.979	3	
750m	46.345	4	14.423
875m	54.074	5	
1000m	1:02.209	6	15.864

Tile that wall

Context
- Students will be familiar with the idea of symmetry.
- This activity encourages them to put their knowledge into practice, in designing an arrangement of wall tiles.

Lesson plan
This activity will take one or two lessons.

Starter
- Students will be familiar with tiles covering walls and floors. Almost certainly, they will have noticed that sometimes these are arranged in patterns.
- The intention of this activity is for students to use a single design of tile to produce a symmetrical design to tile a wall.
- Introduce Task 1 from the Pupil Book. Give each student four of the tiles cut from the template on Worksheet: Tile that wall.
- Ask students to make different arrangements of the tiles, to produce symmetrical patterns. They should sketch their results and describe the types of symmetry they can see.
- Round off with some questions such as:
  - Can anyone show me a pattern with four lines of symmetry?

More detailed guidance
- Let students work with just four tiles at this stage, although you could allow two students to put their eight tiles together to extend a pattern.
- Encourage students to find patterns with different types of symmetry:
  - Can you find a pattern with rotational symmetry but no lines of symmetry?
- The four tiles could be arranged either in a square or in a line of four. The latter is particularly useful for showing translation symmetry.
- Use the questions at the end to ensure that all students are confident about reflection, rotation and translation symmetry. Ask for one example of each type.

Main activity
- Lead in to Task 2 by showing a block of four tiles, from the starter, arranged in a pattern.

Learning objectives

Representing: decide which methods to use to make progress with the solution

Analysing: analyse a pattern or a relationship, using appropriate techniques

Interpreting: give a conclusion or answer to the original problem, using language and forms of presentation that make sense to a wider population

Performing: give a solution to a practical problem, even if it is not within a familiar context, and make sure the solution is presented in a clear and understandable way

APP: evidence for Using and applying mathematics, Shape, space and measures

PLTS: develops Creative thinkers, Reflective learners

Underpinning maths:
reflection, rotation, translation symmetry tessellations

© HarperCollins*Publishers* 2009

 *Rich Task*

- Show how these could be repeated (translated) horizontally and vertically to cover a wall.

Resources
Pupil Book page 112
squared paper
scissors
glue
Worksheet:
Tile that wall

- Ask students to work in pairs to do Task 2. Each pair should design a simple pattern on a tile. Then they will use multiple copies of this to make a pattern to cover a wall. The wall pattern should be symmetrical but the type of symmetry is their choice.
- Give students copies of the blank tiles on page 2 of Worksheet: Tile that wall. These would be best printed on card. The students can cut them up themselves.
- To record their final designs, give students another copy of page 2 of the Worksheet. They could either draw the finished design or glue the tiles in place.

More detailed guidance

- Encourage the students to choose a simple design, using a single colour. Remind them that they will have to make a lot of copies. This is a practical consideration in real life, too. A simple pattern is easier to reproduce and a single colour keeps the cost down.
- Encourage the students to think carefully about the tile design and perhaps try it out before they commit themselves. They should try to imagine what a number of the tiles together will look like.
- A good approach is to start with a block of a small number of tiles; they used four in the starter. Then they should imagine what the pattern will look like if that unit is repeated over the whole wall.

Plenary

- Give students an opportunity to show their tile patterns to the class and describe the symmetries they contain.

More detailed guidance

- An alternative would be for each pair to hold up their pattern and ask other students to describe it.

Rich Task

Extension work
- This work could be extended by asking students to look at patterns on wallpaper, which are often based on repeating blocks and show different types of symmetry.

Outcomes
- Students will have put their knowledge of symmetry to use in designing a pattern based on using a single square tile in different orientations.
- They should have demonstrated that they can talk about symmetry using appropriate language.

© HarperCollins*Publishers* 2009

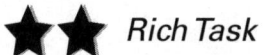 *Rich Task*

Worksheet: Tile that wall

Worksheet: Tile that wall

Rich Task

Body mass index

Context
- The body mass index (BMI) is a measure used to show if an adult is at a healthy weight.
- Students may be familiar with the concept of BMI from PE lessons or from PSHE.

Lesson plan
Starter
- Explain that in this lesson they are going to look at what a **healthy weight** means.
- In particular they are going to look at **body mass index**.
- Check whether students have heard of this and what they already know about it.
- Establish that:
  - BMI is a way of deciding whether an adult is at a healthy weight (the rules for children are more complicated)
  - It is calculated from the person's **weight in kg** and **height in m**.
- Demonstrate the use of an interactive BMI calculator, available on the internet.
- The possible categories are given in the Pupil Book. They are:

18.5–25	healthy
25–30	overweight
> 30	obese
< 18.5	underweight

- Now tell students the formula, which is in the Pupil Book:

  BMI = (weight in kg) ÷ (height in m)^2

- Check that students can use a calculator to get the same answer as the example done on the website calculator. This will check correct use of a calculator and you can also discuss rounding to one decimal place.
  Note: technically we should talk about **mass** rather than **weight** but the latter term is generally used in this context.
- Ask students to do Tasks 1 and 2 in the Pupil Book. This will check they understand and can use the formula. Check their answers.

A	tall thin adult	17.3	underweight
B	short fat adult	31.3	obese
C	'normal' adult	21.0	healthy
D	child	21.5	The value would be described as healthy but the BMI can be misleading for children because of differing growth rates and the effects of puberty.

Learning objectives

Representing: decide which methods to use to make progress with the solution

Analysing: analyse a pattern or a relationship, using appropriate techniques

Interpreting: give a conclusion or answer to the original problem, using language and forms of presentation that make sense to a wider population

Performing: use a range of mathematics to find solutions; check work and methods when tackling a problem and decide if a different approach may be more effective

APP: evidence for Using and applying mathematics, Handling data

PLTS: develops Team workers, Self-managers

Cross-curricular links: Science, ICT, PSHE

© HarperCollins Publishers 2009

Rich Task ★★

More detailed guidance

- Start with a whole-class discussion. Ask questions such as:
  - What do we mean by a healthy weight?
  - What does it depend on? (height, age and gender)
  - Has anyone heard of body mass index?
  - Does anyone know what it is? (a ratio calculated from a person's weight and height)
- Ask students if they know their own weight, in kilograms and height in metres. There is no need to say what they are. Ask if they have some idea of a 'normal' weight and height.
- Many older people (and some students) are more familiar with imperial units. If this comes up in discussion, remind students of the connections but do not go into detail. It will come up later if students do Task 3 in the Pupil Book.
- Make the following points if they do not come up in class discussion.
  - BMI is a measure that only applies to adults and it is calculated from weight and height. Age and gender are not used in the calculation.
  - For children and teenagers, a more complicated method is used that takes gender and age into account.
  - The words **underweight**, **overweight** and **obese** have precise definitions and are not intended to be rude or insulting.
- If you have internet access, search for an interactive BMI calculator. Demonstrate it to the students, using your own height and weight or fictitious data. Measurements can usually be entered in metric or imperial units and both will be displayed simultaneously.
- Explain how the calculation is done. Ask students to use calculators to carry out the same calculation and make sure they get the same answer. The calculator answer will need to be rounded to one decimal place; check that the students understand this.
- Ask students to do Tasks 1 and 2 in the Pupil Book. The point of this is to ensure that they understand the formula and can use a calculator correctly.
- Discuss students' answers and check that they all agree on the correct solutions before moving on to the main activities.

Main activities

Session 1

- Ask students to work in pairs to do Task 3. They are asked to find a possible height and weight for someone who has a BMI of 25 and is on the borderline of being overweight.
- Use a plenary to discuss answers.
  - Are they reasonable?
  - What method was used?

Underpinning maths:
using formulae
trial and improvement
rounding results of calculations
choosing appropriate tables or graphs to represent data
converting imperial units

Resources
Pupil Book page 114
computers
a BMI calculator
(Search the internet for 'BMI calculator'.)
calculators
mini-whiteboards
large sheets of paper for making posters
glue
internet access

© HarperCollins Publishers 2009

 *Rich Task*

More detailed guidance

- If your students use them, mini-whiteboards would be appropriate for this activity.
- Students working at level 2 can initially be set the task without further guidance and only be given suggestions if they are unable to make progress.
- Students working at level 1 will need a more structured introduction. You can give this by modelling an approach to the task, for example, start with the height and weight you used in the starter. Talk through how you could change it. The teacher's side of the dialogue might go something like this:
  - My weight is 60 kg and my height is 1.62 m. What calculation shall I do?'
  - Okay, 60 divided by 1.62 squared. My calculator says 22.862368... How can I round that off?
  - 22.9 is a bit less than the 25 I want. What could I change to make the answer bigger?
  - Make the weight bigger? Okay, what shall I try?

  and so on, using trial and improvement.
- Notice that making the height smaller will **increase** the BMI; to emphasise this you could ask:
  - How could I increase the BMI by changing the height? (make it smaller)
- An alternative to this trial and improvement method would be to rearrange the formula, for example, starting with weight = 25 x (height)² and substituting in a height. Do not tell students this because they do not have to do it that way and it is better to give them a chance to discover it for themselves. You want to avoid giving them an arbitrary rule that they do not understand.
- Have a short plenary at the end of this activity.
- Ask each pair to give you their answers and write them on the board. Do not make any comments at this stage. If the pairs of values are recorded in order of increasing height or weight then patterns and possible errors will be easier to spot.
- When a number of pairs of values are on the board ask:
  - Do they are look reasonable? (Encourage students to look for a pattern: as weight increases so does the height.)
  - Are there any that seem different from the rest? (Do any break the pattern?)
  - Do we need to check any?
- Check and correct if necessary. Emphasise that errors can always occur; checking helps to spot and correct them. Students need to feel confident enough not to be upset by making errors. Ask:
  - Are they all reasonable heights and weights for an adult? (Between 1.5 m and 2.1 m and between 40 kg and 140 kg might be reasonable.)

Session 2

- Ask students to work in groups for Task 4. They are asked to produce a poster that adults can use to decide whether they are at a healthy weight. Assume that the adults will know their own heights and weights.
- Ask students to discuss in their groups how to present the poster. When they have made a decision they can start on the poster.
- Do not tell students what to do but give them as much independence as possible in deciding how to tackle the task. Possible approaches could be:
  - a table of heights and weights; for example, the range of healthy weights for a given height
  - a graph with weight on one axis and height on the other with critical lines added so that a healthy weight is between the lines.
- Other approaches are possible.

© HarperCollins*Publishers* 2009

Rich Task ★★

More detailed guidance
- Make the following points clear.
  - The poster will be used by adults to check their BMI. These are the audience for their writing. (This is a concept that will be familiar from English lessons.)
  - We shall assume the adults know their height and weight in metric units. (The extension work involves asking students to think about imperial units.)
- Give students working at level 2 the opportunity to work independently. Let them make their own decisions unless they are unable to make progress without guidance.
- Students working at level 1 will be less independent and may need a more structured start and more guidance as they carry out the task.
- Here are some suggestions for guidance.
  - Ask how the necessary information could be displayed.
  - Look for answers in the form of a table or a graph.
  - Question students about what the table would look like or what type of graph would be the most appropriate.
  - A simple table might look like this.

Height (m)	Range of healthy weights (kg)		
1.60	47.4	to	64.0
1.65	50.4	to	68.1

  - A graph drawn using a spreadsheet might look like this (note that they are not straight lines).

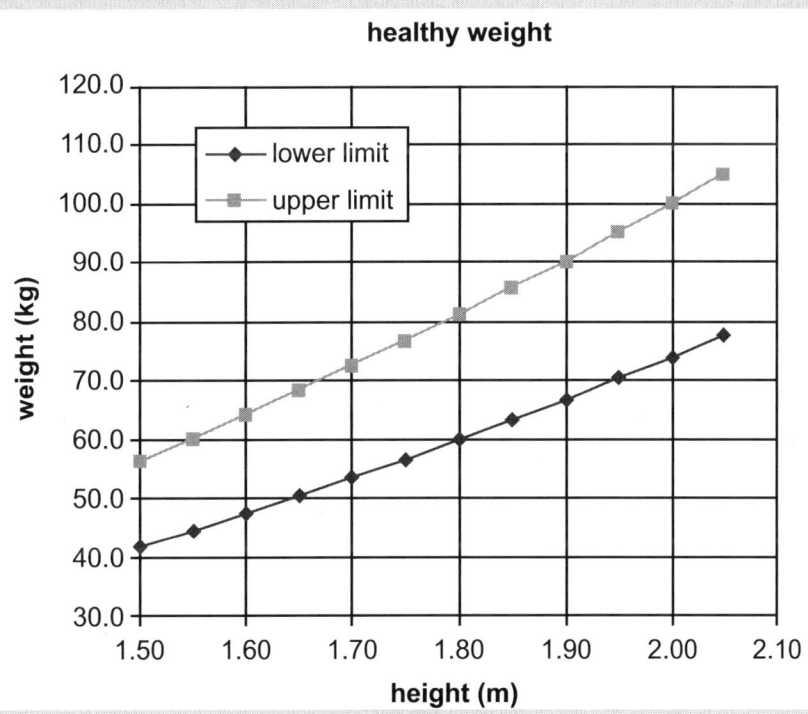

  - Ask how will we get the numbers we need. (Some are already on the board.)
- The poster should also have instructions for how to use it.
- If necessary, give students guidance about sharing the tasks in their groups.
- If necessary, provide large sheets of paper, felt tips, rulers, writing paper, glue.
- If students have access to ICT resources they could use them to produce graphs, charts or tables.

© HarperCollins*Publishers* 2009

 *Rich Task*

Plenaries

- This activity is likely to last more than one lesson.
- Use a plenary at the end of the first lesson to produce a report on progress so far.
- Give each group an opportunity to show their finished poster to the rest of the class and explain how they tackled the task.
- Give students the opportunity to assess how well they have met all of the learning objectives.

More detailed guidance

- One member of the group can be the spokesperson while the others hold up the poster at the front of the class.
- They can say why they chose their method of presentation and justify the range of values they have displayed.
- Go through the learning objectives to the students.
- For each learning objective students should record something they have done and how successful they have been. For example:
  - Decide which methods to use to make progress with a solution.
    I changed the weight until the BMI was 25. I did this successfully in every case.
  - Analyse a pattern or relationship using appropriate techniques.
    I saw that if the weight increases the height does too. I saw that one of the answers on the board was wrong.
  - Give a conclusion or answer to the original problem, using language and forms of presentation that make sense to a wider population.
    I wrote the instructions to go on our poster. I think I gave a clear explanation.
    I thought about the target audience. I did make a spelling mistake.

Extension work

Task 5 (extension)

- Ask students to do Task 5 in the Pupil Book, in which they practise conversion of imperial units.
- Then they can modify their poster for use by adults who only use imperial units.

More detailed guidance

- Task 5 has been set deliberately to involve only feet and stones. When looking at the poster, students could consider either including a conversion table or relabelling the axes. In either case, they will also run into the problem of using inches and pounds.
- The information given in the Pupil Book can be used to convert from imperial to metric. For example, 5 feet 7 inches is 5 × 0.305 + 7 × 0.0254 = 1.70 m. Students will need to be careful to use the correct units here.
- If they choose to use a conversion table they will need to think about how many values to include in the table, while keeping it to a manageable size. For example, going from 7 stone to 20 stone in one-pound intervals is not a sensible idea!

Task 6 (extension)

- Ask students to do Task 6 in the Pupil Book. This shows that a person could be technically obese while still being physically fit.
- Ask students to think of other people who might have an extreme value for their BMI. They can use the internet to investigate this. They should be prepared to present their findings to the class. They could also consider any modifications they might make to their posters in the light of their findings.

Rich Task ★★

More detailed guidance
- Rugby players, particularly forwards, are likely to have high BMI. Other likely candidates are weightlifters, shot-putters and body-builders.
- Some people might have a particularly low BMI. Possibilities include fashion models, actresses and jockeys.
- Finding information could be set as a homework task.
- This topic could lead to an interesting discussion about whether having an extreme BMI is necessarily the same as being unfit. Although BMI is a measure that gives a good guide for the majority of adults, it only takes height and weight into account. Students should know that there are other significant factors to consider, when thinking about fitness, and be aware what they are. Exercise, diet and lifestyle are all important factors.
- A possible addition to their posters would be some indication that BMI is not the only factor to consider when thinking about weight.

Outcomes
- The posters can be displayed in the classroom or around the school.
- Perhaps it may be appropriate to put one up in the staff room.

Green travel

Context
- Students will know that carbon dioxide is a greenhouse gas that contributes to global warming.
- In this activity, students will look at the carbon dioxide emissions involved in journeys they might make.

Lesson plan
This activity may last for one or two lessons.

Starter
- Check that students are aware that carbon dioxide is a greenhouse gas that contributes to global warming.
- Ask if any students travel to school by car.
- Explain that in Task 1 they will look at the carbon dioxide emissions caused by a car in a typical journey to school.
- Ask students to look in the Pupil Book, at the data about carbon dioxide car emissions. Then ask them to make an estimate of the carbon dioxide emission rate of any car they travel in regularly.
- Ask students whose families do not have cars to make estimates about the emissions of cars owned by people they know.
- After a few minutes, show them an online calculator and check the accuracy of one or two estimates.

More detailed guidance
- Check that students understand the units of **grams per kilometre** (g/km). Their estimates will be used for the next task.
- Students might want to adjust their estimates in the light of those checked on the calculator.
- Do not check everyone's answer. It will take too long and an estimate will do just as well as an accurate answer. If they are really keen they can check their estimates in their own time.

Main activities
Session 1
- Introduce Task 2. Tell students they are going to calculate how much carbon dioxide they either produce or save, according to whether they do or do not travel to school by car. Those who do not come by car should imagine they have a chauffeur who brings them to school each day and takes them home again.
- Ask students what they need to know to do this task.
- The answers should be the **emission rate of their vehicle** and the **distance travelled, in km**. If they do not know the distance they travel between home and school, distribute copies of a map of the local area and some pieces of string.
- If students live sufficiently close that driving is not an option, they could imagine they are going to stay with a friend who lives further away.

Learning objectives
Representing: recognise that a real-life problem can be solved using appropriate mathematics

Analysing: find a result or solution to the original problem

Interpreting: check that a conclusion is appropriate and accurate in the context of the original problem

Performing: use mathematical skills and knowledge to make progress on a problem, even if it does not use a routine mathematical procedure; give a solution to a practical problem, even if it is not within a familiar context, and make sure the solution is presented in a clear and understandable way

APP: evidence for Using and applying mathematics, Handling data

PLTS: develops Independent enquirers, Team workers

Underpinning maths:
estimation and rounding
scales on maps

© HarperCollins*Publishers* 2009

Rich Task ★★

- Ask students to estimate the annual amount of carbon dioxide emitted on the school run.

More detailed guidance
- Ask students to consider the following points.
  - How many people are there in the car?
  - Are individual passengers responsible for all the carbon dioxide or only a fraction of it?
  - Is it just the journey to school that counts? Where does the car go afterwards?
  - How many days do they come to school in a year?
- Give the students time to think about the points above by themselves.
- If they do not give the issues sufficient consideration, and come up with too simple an answer, ask them a suitable question to make them reconsider.
- Do not jump in with suggestions too quickly; they should be trying to think of the implications for themselves.
- It would be useful to convert the final answer to kilograms or tonnes and round it sensibly. Check whether students have thought about why a rounded answer is appropriate.

Plenary 1
- Ask students to share their answers.
- Check for units and suitable rounding.
- Ask if students are surprised how big the answer is.

More detailed guidance
- As you record the answers, check the units:
  - What would that be in kilograms?
  - How many tonnes is that?
  and the rounding:
  - Do you think we can be that precise?
- Ask the students to look for any results that are very different from the rest, which may indicate an error.

Session 2
- Introduce Task 3. Students are asked to advise someone who lives in a nearby town or city and regularly travels around Great Britain. She wants to know the comparative cost, in terms of carbon dioxide emissions, of the different types of transport available.
- The journey from London to Edinburgh is a good example to use but students should also work on local journeys.
- The distance from London to Edinburgh, by road, is 661 km.
- Students can work in small groups for this task. The types of transport to consider are car, coach, train and plane.
- Distribute the Data sheet: Green travel and tell students to use the data it contains to help them.
- They will need to make an estimate of the distance travelled by each possible mode of transport. They may not be the same; for example, planes usually take a shorter route than cars. Provide appropriate resources to do this, such as maps, mileage charts, measuring equipment, internet access.

Resources
Pupil Book page 117
maps of the local area
string
mileage charts
measuring equipment
information about carbon emissions
(Source: the internet)
internet access
Data sheet: Green travel

© HarperCollins*Publishers* 2009

 *Rich Task*

More detailed guidance

- Depending on how good the transport links in your area are, you could base the work on your own area or choose a different home town or city, such as London, that has good rail links. If there is an airport nearby that will be even better. If there is no airport, you could imagine that there is for the sake of making a comparison.
- You could allocate destinations to students or let them choose. They do not need all to be different. Make any necessary assumptions about rail, coach or air links.
- Have the equipment available in the room but do not distribute it. Let students decide what they need.
- The Data sheet gives emissions as **kg CO_2 per passenger per km**. Make sure students are aware of what this means. They are based on the average number of passengers per trip.
- A possible extension task is for students to take journey times into account when making recommendations to the client.

Plenary 2

- Ask different groups to explain their findings and recommendations.
  - What seems to be the best choice?
  - What other things are taken into account when choosing the mode of travel?
  - Was the model a good one?
  - How might it be improved?

More detailed guidance

- Other factors to take into account when choosing how to travel include cost, journey time and the time at which you wish to travel.
- There have been simplifications in this model. For example, how realistic are the figures in the Data sheet? They are based on the average number of passengers but of course this can vary. Other sources may give different figures.
- Travelling by car will be more expensive than it appears as it will involve a journey that would not otherwise have taken place. All the carbon dioxide will be 'extra'. By contrast, scheduled public transport will travel whether the client takes it or not and there is no extra cost involved.
- The most efficient method would be if all public transport ran at close to maximum capacity.

Outcomes

- Students will appreciate that simplifications are made in order to tackle a complicated problem.
- They will make appropriate estimates and give solutions to an appropriate degree of accuracy.
- They will have the opportunity to select and use appropriate information to tackle a problem.

Rich Task

Data sheet: Green travel

Carbon Emission Assumptions (10 September 2008)

Kilograms of CO_2 per passenger per kilometre (public transport)

Air journeys	0.1753
Bus journeys	0.1073
Coach journeys	0.029
Light Rail journeys	0.078
Tyne & Wear Metro journeys	0.1207
Docklands Light Rail journeys	0.074
Croydon Tramlink journeys	0.042
Manchester Metrolink journeys	0.0421
Rail journeys	0.0602
London Underground journeys	0.065
Ferry journeys	0.1152

Source: DEFRA, the Department for Environment, Food and Rural Affairs

Turn up the volume

Context
- Students should be familiar with how to calculate the volume of a cuboid (rectangular box) and perhaps of other solid objects.
- In this activity, they are asked to think about something more complicated.

Lesson plan
- Ask the students to bring in empty cuboid packaging, such as cereal boxes; they can be flattened for transporting and then reconstructed.

Starter
- Hold up a cereal box, or similar, and ask students how they could find the volume.
- Ask a pair of students to make any measurements suggested and model the calculation on the board, using a calculator if necessary.
- Make sure everyone clearly understands what to do and the units of the answer. Discuss how much to round the answer.
- Give each pair of students a cereal box of their own and ask them to find the volume. This is Task 1 in the Pupil Book.
- Take feedback from a few groups and discuss whether the answers have been rounded sensibly.

More detailed guidance
- Make sure that students understand that they must take three measurements and multiply the numbers together. A good way to explain it is to say that first they find the area of the base (multiply two sides) and then multiply by the height.
- If any students are confused about this, have a cuboid made up of cubes available so that they can see the number of cubes on the base (length multiplied by width) and the number of layers (height).
- Give a cereal box and a ruler or measuring tape to a pair of students and ask them to make the necessary measurements. The class can then make the necessary calculations and you can model them at the same time.
- Emphasise the correct units. If the measurements are in centimetres then the volume will be in cubic centimetres (cm^3). Centimetres are the appropriate units for this exercise.
- If someone uses millimetres (mm) for their measurements, this would be an opportunity to discuss different possible units.
- Students will need to consider the accuracy of the measuring.
    - Consider a box that measures 5.5 cm, 9.1 cm and 25.1 cm.
    - If students measure these dimensions as 5.5, 9 and 25 the answer will be 1237.5 cm^3.
    - If they use the more exact figures the answer is 1256.255 cm^3.

Learning objectives

Representing: decide how to show the initial problem, using mathematical symbols; decide which methods to use to make progress with the solution

Analysing: use appropriate mathematical procedures

Interpreting: check that a conclusion is appropriate and accurate in the context of the original problem

Performing: use mathematical skills and knowledge to make progress on a problem, even if it does not use a routine mathematical procedure

APP: evidence for Using and applying mathematics, Shape, space and measures

PLTS: develops Creative thinkers, Team workers

Underpinning maths:
calculate the volume of a cuboid
formulae for other shapes such as cylinders
units of volume
estimation

© HarperCollinsPublishers 2009

Rich Task

- Students are often surprised at how big the difference is. Both answers need to be rounded.
- A useful rule is that the answer cannot be accurate to more significant figures than are the numbers you start with.
- Rounding to three significant figures will give 1240 and 1260. Rounding to two significant figures will give 1200 and 1300.
- The depth of detail to which you go with your students depends on their ability. The key point for students to appreciate is that some rounding is sensible but they need not get distracted by too much detail.

• When students find the volumes of their own boxes (Task 1), there is no need to check them all. Ask each pair to compare their answer with that of another pair and see if their answers seem reasonable.
  - Has the smaller one got the smaller volume?
  - If they look roughly the same size do the calculations confirm that?
  Any figures that look unreasonable can then be checked.

• When taking feedback concentrate on discussing the sensible rounding of answers but note that this is another opportunity to check that all the answers are reasonable.

Resources
Pupil Book page 119
selection of cereal boxes or similar containers
measuring equipment, particularly rulers and tape measures
large sheets of paper and felt tip pens

Main activities

Session 1

- Ask students to look at Task 2 in the Pupil Book.
- Explain that the task is to find the volume of a person. Ask them to spend a couple of minutes, in twos or threes, discussing how they could do this. Then take feedback.
- The following are possible suggestions that may arise.
  - Treat a person as a box to get an approximate answer.
  - Think of the different parts of a body as separate boxes (or cylinders or spheres) and add them together.
  - Jump in a bath full of water and measure the overflow.
- Do not suggest methods to students but encourage them to come up with their own.
- Students should continue to work in groups of two or three.
- Clarify which person's volume they are going to find. Any method is going to require some measurement. Not all students will be comfortable with having their measurements taken and it may be necessary to estimate an average person or use the teacher.
- Make it clear at the start that, at the end, each group will be asked to report back to the class about how they tackled this problem.

More detailed guidance

- If you can find a large box (perhaps from a sizeable piece of electrical equipment) use this as a starting point. Ask:
  - Could you fit inside this box?
  - If we know the volume of the box, what can we say about your volume?
  - It must be less; can we say how much less?
- If no such a box is available, ask a student to sit on a desk and ask the class to imagine a box enclosing this volunteer.

© HarperCollins*Publishers* 2009

 *Rich Task*

- Give the students time to make suggestions for finding the volume of a person. You could naively ask if we can just multiply width, depth and height for a person to get the volume and if not, why not. (Because a person is not a box!) It does not matter how wild their ideas are at this stage.
- Put the students in groups of two or three. Their task is to find the volume of a person. Be aware that although volume is not such a sensitive issue as weight, finding the volume of their own body may be uncomfortable for some students. Consider this when arranging the groups. You could always volunteer yourself as the victim if there are no other options.
- Students should be allowed to choose their own method; do not direct them to a particular approach. However, the plan must be practicable – which will rule out baths of water or dissection.
- Ask them to spend a few minutes planning what they are going to do; this is always worthwhile. Tell them not to start until you give them the go-ahead. Try to avoid telling them how to improve their plans. It is much better to let them find this out for themselves.
- For students who cannot get started or are not used to working in this way, have some prepared questions ready that will give them more guidance; for example:
  - Imagine a box that is just big enough to stand up in. What size would it be?
  - What could I do to improve the estimate?
- The answers (in cm^3) are likely to be large, in the tens or hundreds of thousands. Students are unlikely to choose to work in metres.
- Make clear that students will be asked to report back to the class on how they worked out their answer. It might be best for them to work on a large sheet of poster paper so that they can display their work.
- One possible method would involve modelling different parts of the body separately: trunk, legs, arms, head and so on. This could involve cylinders and spheres, if students know how to find the volumes of those shapes, but they are not essential; they are not even necessarily more accurate. It will not be 'better' just because the mathematical tools used are more complicated.
- Students who complete the task could be asked to consider ways of refining and improving their estimate; alternatively they could go on to the extension activities, Task 3 or Task 4 in the Pupil Book.

Plenary part 1

- Ask groups to give their answers and explain their methods.
- Bring out the point that any answer is an estimate and it is not practical to find an exact answer. Ask whether they took this into account when giving their answers.

More detailed guidance

- The methods that the students used are more important than the details of any calculations they carried out.
- Keep the presentations brief so that you can get round the whole class.
- Students often fail to appreciate the need to round an answer that is only an estimate. Be prepared to ask students if they think their answers need to be rounded.
- After the last presentation you could lead into the final evaluation by asking:
  - Did any of you see something in someone else's presentation that you thought was a good idea?

Rich Task ★★★

Plenary part 2: final evaluation
- After the plenary presentations ask each group to think about the task they have completed and the presentations they have seen. Ask them to answer these questions.
  - How successfully did you complete the task?
  - How confident are you that you have made a good estimate of the volume?
  - If you did the task again, what changes would you make?
- Allow sufficient time to complete this.
- Ask one or two students to read their evaluation to the rest of the class at the end.

Tasks 3 and 4 (extension)
- Ask students to do Task 3 in the Pupil Book, estimating the volume of Robert Earl Hughes.
- Ask students to do Task 4 in the Pupil Book, estimating the volume of a baby.

More detailed guidance
- The extension tasks could be set for students as they complete the main activity or they could be used as activities for the whole class. In the latter case, follow up with a plenary on the same lines as the main activity, although you may not wish to use posters in this case. Once again the emphasis is on the process used and appreciating that the answer is an estimate and not exact.
- Task 4 could be done by the total immersion method but students should be **discouraged** from trying this at home!

Outcomes
- Students will extend their knowledge of mathematics to apply it an unfamiliar situation.
- Students will make a presentation to the class.
- Students will evaluate how successfully they have carried out the task.

© HarperCollins*Publishers* 2009

Give us a job

Context
- Students are interested in earning money but they are often unaware of the expenses that they will encounter when they get a job and leave home.
- It is important that they can manage their spending and live within their means. They need to think about the amount of money they might be earning and the expenses they will have in living away from home.
- This activity will give them an opportunity to use their number skills in a realistic context.

Lesson plan
- This activity could last two or three lessons.
- The approach is to give students the details of a job, chosen at random.
- They will be asked to plan how they will spend their money.
- At regular intervals, extra constraints such as tax, accommodation, food and utilities will be added in, which will gradually reduce the available income and require spending plans to be modified.

Starter
- Explain that students are going to do an activity that will help them to plan their expenditure when they leave school.
- Start by allocating them each a job. Give out the cards from Data sheet: Give us a job at this point, one per student. The salary may be given per hour, per day or per annum (pa).
- Ask the students to carry out Task 1 in the Pupil Book, in which they work out their weekly pay and then list some things they will spend it on. Their plans are likely to be extravagant at this stage but reality will gradually take over as the activity progresses. They need to keep a record of their plans and any changes they make as we move through this unit.

More detailed guidance
- The data on the cards was taken from advertisements for jobs in Birmingham on one day in 2009. You may wish to replace them with jobs taken from your local area, perhaps using an internet search.
- In Task 1, students work out their weekly salary. Where the salary is per annum they will divide by 52. They should round the answer sensibly.
- Where payment is per day you can assume a working week of five days. An added complication is that they will not be paid for holidays! You could throw this in as an extra consideration later if you wish.
- Where payment is per hour they will need to assume a sensible working week of perhaps about 35 hours. People on hourly rates usually (but not always) get holiday pay.

Learning objectives
Representing: decide which methods to use to make progress with the solution
Analysing: find a result or solution to the original problem
Interpreting: check that a conclusion is appropriate and accurate in the context of the original problem
Performing: draw a conclusion from working and provide a mathematical justification for this conclusion

APP: evidence for Using and applying mathematics, Calculating

PLTS: develops Self-managers, Reflective learners

Cross-curricular links: ICT, PSHE, Citizenship

Underpinning maths:
calculations involving time and money
approximation and estimation
using a calculator to find percentages

© HarperCollins*Publishers* 2009

Rich Task

Main activities
Session 1
- Move on to Task 2, adding the first constraint of income tax and national insurance. Do not go into all the complications here; the students can quickly get a reasonable estimate of what they will pay and that is all they need.
- Give them these formulae:
  income tax = 20% of (weekly income − £124)
  national insurance = 11% of (weekly income − £110)
- If they are earning less than £110 a week they do not pay anything.
- Ask the students to work out their deductions and adjust their disposable weekly income.
- Now ask them to revise their spending plans. Can they still afford everything?

Resources
Pupil Book page 121
a set of job cards either from Data sheet: Give us a job or taken from local data
details of accommodation to rent from local newspapers or websites
internet access

More detailed guidance
- The tax and NI figures are for the 2009–10 tax year. Current figures can be found online. None of the jobs given will take them into the higher tax bracket.
- NI ignores possible exceptional circumstances but that does not matter for this exercise.

Session 2
- Introduce Task 3. Tell the students that they will be living away from home and they are going to share a house or flat with friends. They have the task of finding accommodation at a price they can afford. To do this they will need details of property available in the area. Make available details of local property from websites, from newspapers or from any local letting agencies.
- Ask what impact this will have on their spending.

More detailed guidance
- There are plenty of websites for rented accommodation, including the gum tree sites, which use a district in the name, such as Bristol.gumtree.com.
- Sometimes student accommodation is better value, even if they are not 'students'.
- The cost of accommodation will be shared by the occupants, so students will need to take that into account when making their choice.
- Local data is most meaningful to students. They may find that, to fit their budget, they need to live in a less desirable neighbourhood.
- Groups of students could imagine that they are going to live together. They could work together to look for suitable accommodation to share.

Session 3
- Task 4 reminds the students that they need to eat. Students now need to estimate how much they will need to spend on food. Discuss how they could approach this.
- Here are some suggestions.
  - Look on the internet.
  - Find out what their family spends in a week on food.
  - Look at the cost of a week's worth of takeaways.
  - Ask a sample of people what they spend.
  - Cost out a notional week's shopping.
  - Record what you eat in a day and try to cost it.

© HarperCollins*Publishers* 2009

 *Rich Task*

- The students can work in pairs to do this. The important point is that they should be able to explain and justify their conclusions.

More detailed guidance
- There is no right answer to this question; the desired outcome will be reasonable estimates that each student can justify.
- One way to tackle this is to start with answers that are clearly too small or too big. So £10 a week is not enough; £200 is more than enough. So somewhere in between…

Plenary after session 3
- Ask students for their estimates for food costs, with reasons, and see what sort of variation there is. Students may wish to adjust their own estimates on the basis of what they hear other students say.
- Now ask students to review the progress so far.
   - Are they running out of money or can they still afford a night out at the weekend?
   - Was that house or flat too expensive?
   - Do they need to move somewhere cheaper?

More detailed guidance
- The intention of this activity is to encourage the students to listen to the arguments made by others and review their decision in the light of what they hear. This is a skill they need to develop. Ask explicit questions such as:
   - Are you convinced by Ann's argument?
   - Do you want to change your estimate on the basis of what you have heard?
  to foster this.
- Praise the quality of their justifications, not the answers.
- Give the students time to think about whether to make changes. If they are unwilling to do so, warn them that more expenses are on the way.

Session 4
- Start Task 5 by asking students what else they have not considered yet. This could include mobile phone, clothes, council tax, water rates, heating and lighting, transport, household items and leisure activities.
- Say that they can assume that council tax and water rates are included in the rent (as is sometimes the case).
- Now ask the students to make estimates of the other expense items.
- If anyone mentions running a car, say that they will look at that separately as the final task.

More detailed guidance
- Once again, students will find it difficult to estimate some items. However, they should be encouraged to make estimates and to justify them if they can.
- Electricity and gas bills are calculated quarterly so students will need to work out how to find a weekly cost from that. These bills also vary according to the time of year.
- Mobile phone tariffs are usually charged monthly so, again, they will probably need to work out the weekly equivalent.
- Talk to students individually, as they work on this, and ask them to explain their reasons for particular items.

© HarperCollins*Publishers* 2009

Rich Task ★★★

Plenary after session 4
- Ask the students how the process has gone.
  - Has anyone run out of money?
  - How much did they have to change their original plans?
  - Are they surprised by the final result?
- Ask for feedback from students who had the highest and lowest salaries, to see what differences there are.

More detailed guidance
- Students will probably be surprised by how quickly what seems like a good salary will disappear when all the costs are taken into account.
- Many people who go straight from school to work continue to live at home initially. Students should now be able to see why.

Task 6 (extension)
- As an extra activity, students could try Task 6, deciding whether they can afford to run a car.
- The costs will include insurance, road tax, fuel (which depends on likely mileage), servicing and breakdown or repair costs.
- Researching all these is a substantial task but a lot of the information can be found on the internet.

More detailed guidance
- This could be done as a stand-alone task at a different time.
- Students often consider just the cost of the car and do not appreciate how much more they will need to pay.
- The cost of running a car is easier to calculate on an annual basis. Then this can be converted into a weekly figure.
- The task deliberately does not specify the model of car. If students are likely to find this task difficult you could suggest a model to use or ask them to think what sort of car a granddad might drive.
- Breakdown or repair costs are difficult to estimate because there is a random element involved. You could expect the chance of such repair to increase with the age of the car.

Outcomes
- Students have had the opportunity to break down the substantial task of budgeting to live on a salary into more manageable parts.
- They have had the opportunity to estimate and approximate costs, to justify them and to review their conclusions in the light of discussion with others.
- They may have had to adjust their spending and reconsider their priorities if they found they were running out of money.
- They should have been checking their calculations at each stage of the process.

© HarperCollins*Publishers* 2009

 *Rich Task*

Data sheet 1: Give us a job, job cards

All these jobs were advertised in Birmingham on one day in 2009.

Freight sales coordinator £14 000 pa	Payroll officer £15 000 pa	Occupational therapist £25 per hour	Care worker £9 per hour
Technical sales engineer £30 000 pa	Sales executive £22 000 pa	Accountant £29 000	Catering assistant £5.75 per hour
Conference assistant £6 per hour	Ledger clerk £18 000 pa	Asbestos analyst £19 000 pa	Reception class teacher £120 per day
Beauty clinic manager £32 000 pa	Accounts clerk £7.60 per hour	Ultrasound operator £27 000	Financial adviser £18 400
Security adviser £20 000 pa	Engineering performance assessor £21 000 pa	Mortgage adviser £24 000	Recruitment consultant £17 500
Hardware sales executive £19 400 pa	Personal injury paralegal £20 400 pa	Physiotherapist £22 per hour	Human resources adviser £26 000
Social care worker £14 700 pa	Investigator (anti money laundering) £8.50 per hour	Teacher of mathematics £140 per day	CCTV engineer £24 000 pa
Events and sales executive £16 200 pa	Insurance broker £18 600 pa	Speech therapist £21 per hour	Maintenance technician £26 500 pa
Bank customer adviser £12 400 pa	Assistant financial analyst £9.50 per hour	Office manager £20 500 pa	Motor claims handler £16 500 pa
Packaging designer £16 per hour	Sous chef in a restaurant £23 000 pa	Call centre operator £14 500 pa	Nursery manager £19 500 pa
Fundraising coordinator £20 500 pa	Personal trainer £17 000 pa	Telemarketer researcher £1300 pa	Maintenance engineer £26 500 pa
Social worker £21 per hour	SEN teaching assistant £10 per hour	Secretary £7.50 per hour	Assistant restaurant manager £18 500 pa

© HarperCollins*Publishers* 2009

Populations

Context
- Students may have looked at population issues in other subjects.
- This activity will give them a clearer understanding of relative sizes of countries and populations.

Lesson plan
This activity will last two or three lessons.

Starter
- Explain to students that they are going to carry out an investigation involving the populations and areas of some countries. An important way of comparing countries is to work out the population density.
- Demonstrate how to work out the population density of the classroom you are in. First, calculate the area. It will be sensible to take some measurements beforehand. Do not get tied up in details.
- The area will be in square metres. Divide the number of people in the room by the area, to get the population density of the room in **people per m²**.
- Ask some questions to ensure students understand that this is a measure of how full the room is.
- Ask students to do Task 1 in the Pupil Book. The units this time will be **people per km²**. After a few minutes, check the answers students have found.

More detailed guidance
- This will be an introduction to an investigation in which the students decide on a question or hypothesis to explore. They will be looking at the relationship between population and area for different countries.
- Population density is a measure that is often used and students may be aware of it from geography or humanities lessons. The starter is intended to ensure that students are familiar with this concept so that they can use it if they wish.
- The population density of the classroom is likely to be less than one. The calculator answer will need to be rounded sensibly; take the opportunity to ensure that students are clear about how to do this.
- Population density is an average figure and therefore it does not give any information about variations in different parts of the country; for example, how crowded the cities are. It can be loosely thought of as a measure of 'how crowded' a country is but, of course, regional variations affect how crowded it actually feels at any particular place.

Learning objectives

Representing: decide how to represent the problem to make it easier to solve using mathematics

Analysing: use appropriate mathematical procedures

Interpreting: interpret results and solutions and make a generalisation about them

Performing: analyse the situation or problem and decide which is the appropriate mathematical method needed to tackle it; check work and methods when tackling a problem and decide if a different approach may be more effective

APP: evidence for Using and applying mathematics, Calculating

PLTS: develops Independent enquirers, Reflective learners

Cross-curricular links: ICT, Geography

Underpinning maths:
carry out calculations in practical contexts
use equations
know how to choose a suitable format and scale to fit data

© HarperCollins*Publishers* 2009

 *Rich Task*

Main activity: an investigation

- Distribute Resource sheet: Populations and explain that it lists the populations and areas of all the countries in the world. As you do so, explain that you want them to think about how they could use it. Set Task 2 from the Pupil Book. Students could work in pairs. Give them enough time to complete this task fully.
- Bring the class together to discuss their suggestions.
- Introduce Task 3 (the investigation). Students should decide what they want to investigate (from Task 2) and what information they need. They should back up their conclusions with suitable charts and calculations. Working in pairs would encourage discussion.
- Decide the form in which their work should be presented. A poster could be displayed on the wall afterwards.

> **Resources**
> Pupil Book page 123
> computers
> ICT resources
> internet access
> Data sheet: Populations

More detailed guidance

- Encourage students to use a subset of the available data that is appropriate to their investigation. The sheet contains more information than they need and part of the exercise is for them to choose what is appropriate.
- Students will be able to work more efficiently and effectively if they have access to the data on a spreadsheet. The spreadsheet can then be used for sorting, editing calculations and creating appropriate charts.
- Students should be able to calculate the population densities, using a spreadsheet if possible, and use that as well as the figures for population and area.

Plenary

- Use a plenary to give students the opportunity to describe and discuss their findings with the rest of the class.

More detailed guidance

- Making posters would allow students to explain their findings to other students. Alternatively they may be able to do this using some form of ICT or other presentation.

Extension work

- If extension work is required, students could be asked to consider the limitations of using population density as a measure of 'crowdedness'. For example, Scotland has a lower population density than England but this masks the fact that the highlands are relatively empty and the density in the area including Edinburgh and Glasgow, where a large proportion of the population lives, is much greater.
- Figures for different regions of England could give an idea of internal variations.

Outcomes

- To do the investigation students will need to select appropriate procedures and tools, including ICT.
- They will make and test conjectures and have opportunities to generalise.
- The will record methods and conclusions and present a reasoned argument, using diagrams or graphs.

© HarperCollins*Publishers* 2009

Data sheet: Populations

Country	Population	Area(sq km)
Afghanistan	33 609 937	647 500
Akrotiri	15 700	123
Albania	3 639 453	28 748
Algeria	34 178 188	2 381 740
American Samoa	65 628	199
Andorra	83 888	468
Angola	12 799 293	1 246 700
Anguilla	14 436	102
Antigua and Barbuda	85 632	443
Argentina	40 913 584	2 766 890
Armenia	2 967 004	29 743
Aruba	103 065	193
Australia	21 262 641	7 686 850
Austria	8 210 281	83 870
Azerbaijan	8 238 672	86 600
Bahamas The	309 156	13 940
Bahrain	727 785	665
Bangladesh	156 050 883	144 000
Barbados	284 589	431
Belarus	9 648 533	207 600
Belgium	10 414 336	30 528
Belize	307 899	22 966
Benin	8 791 832	112 620
Bermuda	67 837	53
Bhutan	691 141	47 000
Bolivia	9 775 246	1 098 580
Bosnia and Herzegovina	4 613 414	51 209
Botswana	1 990 876	600 370
Brazil	198 739 269	8 511 965
British Virgin Islands	24 491	153
Brunei	388 190	5 770
Bulgaria	7 204 687	110 910
Burkina Faso	15 746 232	274 200
Burma	48 137 741	678 500
Burundi	8 988 091	27 830
Cambodia	14 494 293	181 040
Cameroon	18 879 301	475 440
Canada	33 487 208	9 984 670
Cape Verde	429 474	4 033
Cayman Islands	49 035	262
Central African Republic	4 511 488	622 984
Chad	10 329 208	1 284 000
Chile	16 601 707	756 950
China	1 338 612 968	9 596 960
Christmas Island	1 402	135
Cocos (Keeling) Islands	596	14
Colombia	45 644 023	1 138 910
Comoros	752 438	2 170

© HarperCollinsPublishers 2009

 Rich Task

Country	Population	Area
Congo, Democratic Republic of the	68 692 542	2 345 410
Congo, Republic of the	4 012 809	342 000
Cook Islands	11 870	237
Costa Rica	4 253 877	51 100
Cote d'Ivoire	20 617 068	322 460
Croatia	4 489 409	56 542
Cuba	11 451 652	110 860
Cyprus	796 740	9 250
Czech Republic	10 211 904	78 866
Denmark	5 500 510	43 094
Dhekelia	15 700	131
Djibouti	516 055	23 000
Dominica	72 660	754
Dominican Republic	9 650 054	48 730
Ecuador	14 573 101	283 560
Egypt	83 082 869	1 001 450
El Salvador	7 185 218	21 040
Equatorial Guinea	633 441	28 051
Eritrea	5 647 168	121 320
Estonia	1 299 371	45 226
Ethiopia	85 237 338	1 127 127
European Union	491 582 852	4 324 782
Falkland Islands (Islas Malvinas)	3 140	12 173
Faroe Islands	48 856	1 399
Fiji	944 720	18 270
Finland	5 250 275	338 145
France	64 057 792	643 427
French Polynesia	287 032	4 167
Gabon	1 514 993	267 667
Gambia, The	1 782 893	11 300
Gaza Strip	1 551 859	360
Georgia	4 615 807	69 700
Germany	82 329 758	357 021
Ghana	23 832 495	239 460
Gibraltar	28 034	7
Greece	10 737 428	131 940
Greenland	57 600	2 166 086
Grenada	90 739	344
Guam	178 430	541
Guatemala	13 276 517	108 890
Guernsey	65 870	78
Guinea	10 057 975	245 857
Guinea-Bissau	1 533 964	36 120
Guyana	772 298	214 970
Haiti	9 035 536	27 750
Holy See (Vatican City)	826	0
Honduras	7 792 854	112 090
Hong Kong	7 055 071	1 092
Hungary	9 905 596	93 030
Iceland	306 694	103 000
India	1 166 079 217	3 287 590

Rich Task

Indonesia	240 271 522	1 919 440
Iran	66 429 284	1 648 000
Iraq	28 945 657	437 072
Ireland	4 203 200	70 280
Isle of Man	76 512	572
Israel	7 233 701	20 770
Italy	58 126 212	301 230
Jamaica	2 825 928	10 991
Japan	127 078 679	377 835
Jersey	91 626	116
Jordan	6 342 948	92 300
Kazakhstan	15 399 437	2 717 300
Kenya	39 002 772	582 650
Kiribati	112 850	811
Korea North	22 665 345	120 540
Korea South	48 508 972	98 480
Kosovo	1 804 838	10 887
Kuwait	2 691 158	17 820
Kyrgyzstan	5 431 747	198 500
Laos	6 834 942	236 800
Latvia	2 231 503	64 589
Lebanon	4 017 095	10 400
Lesotho	2 130 819	30 355
Liberia	3 441 790	111 370
Libya	6 310 434	1 759 540
Liechtenstein	34 761	160
Lithuania	3 555 179	65 300
Luxembourg	491 775	2 586
Macau	559 846	28
Macedonia	2 066 718	25 333
Madagascar	20 653 556	587 040
Malawi	14 268 711	118 480
Malaysia	25 715 819	329 750
Maldives	396 334	300
Mali	12 666 987	1 240 000
Malta	405 165	316
Marshall Islands	64 522	181
Mauritania	3 129 486	1 030 700
Mauritius	1 284 264	2 040
Mayotte	223 765	374
Mexico	111 211 789	1 972 550
Micronesia Federated States of	107 434	702
Moldova	4 320 748	33 843
Monaco	32 965	2
Mongolia	3 041 142	1 564 116
Montenegro	672 180	14 026
Montserrat	5 097	102
Morocco	34 859 364	446 550
Mozambique	21 669 278	801 590
Namibia	2 108 665	825 418
Nauru	14 019	21

 *Rich Task*

Nepal	28 563 377	147 181
Netherlands	16 715 999	41 526
Netherlands Antilles	227 049	960
New Caledonia	227 436	19 060
New Zealand	4 213 418	268 680
Nicaragua	5 891 199	129 494
Niger	15 306 252	1 267 000
Nigeria	149 229 090	923 768
Niue	1 398	260
Norfolk Island	2 141	35
Northern Mariana Islands	88 662	477
Norway	4 660 539	323 802
Oman	3 418 085	212 460
Pakistan	176 242 949	803 940
Palau	20 796	458
Panama	3 360 474	78 200
Papua New Guinea	6 057 263	462 840
Paraguay	6 995 655	406 750
Peru	29 546 963	1 285 220
Philippines	97 976 603	300 000
Pitcairn Islands	48	47
Poland	38 482 919	312 679
Portugal	10 707 924	92 391
Puerto Rico	3 971 020	13 790
Qatar	833 285	11 437
Romania	22 215 421	237 500
Russia	140 041 247	17 075 200
Rwanda	10 473 282	26 338
Saint Barthelemy	7 448	21
Saint Helena	7 637	413
Saint Kitts and Nevis	40 131	261
Saint Lucia	160 267	616
Saint Martin	29 820	54
Saint Pierre and Miquelon	7 051	242
Saint Vincent and the Grenadines	104 574	389
Samoa	219 998	2 944
San Marino	30 324	61
Sao Tome and Principe	212 679	1 001
Saudi Arabia	28 686 633	2 149 690
Senegal	13 711 597	196 190
Serbia	10 159 046	77 474
Seychelles	87 476	455
Sierra Leone	6 440 053	71 740
Singapore	4 657 542	693
Slovakia	5 463 046	48 845
Slovenia	2 005 692	20 273
Solomon Islands	595 613	28 450
Somalia	9 832 017	637 657
South Africa	49 052 489	1 219 912
Spain	40 525 002	504 782
Sri Lanka	21 324 791	65 610

© HarperCollins*Publishers* 2009

Rich Task

Sudan	41 087 825	2 505 810
Suriname	481 267	163 270
Svalbard	2 116	61 020
Swaziland	1 123 913	17 363
Sweden	9 059 651	449 964
Switzerland	7 604 467	41 290
Syria	20 178 485	185 180
Taiwan	22 974 347	35 980
Tajikistan	7 349 145	143 100
Tanzania	41 048 532	945 087
Thailand	65 905 410	514 000
Timor-Leste	1 131 612	15 007
Togo	6 019 877	56 785
Tokelau	1 416	10
Tonga	120 898	748
Trinidad and Tobago	1 229 953	5 128
Tunisia	10 486 339	163 610
Turkey	76 805 524	780 580
Turkmenistan	4 884 887	488 100
Turks and Caicos Islands	22 942	430
Tuvalu	12 373	26
Uganda	32 369 558	236 040
Ukraine	45 700 395	603 700
United Arab Emirates	4 798 491	83 600
United Kingdom	61 113 205	244 820
United States	307 212 123	9 826 630
Uruguay	3 494 382	176 220
Uzbekistan	27 606 007	447 400
Vanuatu	218 519	12 200
Venezuela	26 814 843	912 050
Vietnam	86 967 524	329 560
Virgin Islands	109 825	1 910
Wallis and Futuna	15 289	274
West Bank	2 461 267	5 860
Western Sahara	405 210	266 000
Yemen	23 822 783	527 970
Zambia	11 862 740	752 614
Zimbabwe	11 392 629	390 580
World	6 706 993 152	510 072 000

Source: www.cia.gov April 2009

Matching charts

New Maths Frameworking 3-Year Scheme of Work

This matches the activities to the topics students will need to have covered to be able to tackle them. However, you need to think about the ability of your students and their stage of development. A good approach could be to use the activities a topic or two later to recall, revise and consolidate learning.

YEAR 7				Assessment
Term 1	**Algebra 1**	**Number 1**	**Geometry and Measures 1** Bridges (**)	Test 1
	Number 2 Money matters 1: Pay (*)	**Statistics 1** Endangered species (*) Stickers (**)	**Algebra 2**	Test 2
Term 2	**Geometry and Measures 2**	**Statistics 2** Deliveries (*)	**Number and Measures 3**	Test 3
	Algebra 3 Rugby numbers (*)	**Geometry and Measures 3**	**Number 4** Money matters 2: Tax and national insurance (**)	Test 4
Term 3	**Algebra 4**	**Geometry and Measures 4** Brick laying patterns (*)	**Statistics 3** Water (*)	Test 5
	Number 5 Darts (*)	**Algebra 5** At the gym (**) Give us a job (***)	**Geometry and Measures 5** Tile that wall (**)	End of year test
YEAR 8				Assessment
Term 1	**Number & Algebra 1** Time zones (**)	**Geometry and Measures 1**		Test 1
	Statistics 1	**Number 2** Money matters 3: Loans and APR (**) Money matters 4: Savings and AER (**)	**Algebra 2**	Test 2
Term 2	**Geometry and Measures 2** Saving energy (***) Turn up the volume (***)	**Algebra 3** Bike race (**)	**Number 3** Football (*) Growing, growing, grown… (***)	Test 3
	Geometry and Measures 3	**Algebra 4**	**Statistics 2** Climate change (***)	Test 4
Term 3	**Number 4** Timetables (***)	**Algebra 5**	**Solving problems**	Test 5
	Geometry and Measures 4 Safe flying over the UK (*) Join a group (*) Paving (*)	**Statistics 3** Shuffleboard (**) Follow that car (*)		End of year test
YEAR 9				Assessment
Term 1	**Algebra 1 & 2** Revision planning (**)	**Number 1** Money matters 5: Mortgages (**)		Test 1
	Algebra 3 Recipes (***)	**Geometry and Measures 1**	**Statistics 1** Stopping distances (***) Body mass index (**)	Test 2
Term 2	**Geometry and Measures 2**	**Number 2**		Test 3
	Algebra 4 Alcohol (***)	**Statistics 2** Wales (*)	**Geometry and Measures 3** Green travel (**) Venting gas appliances (***) Garden designer (***) Planning a bedroom (***)	Test 4
Term 3	**Statistics 3** Populations (***)	**Statistics 4**	**Algebra 5**	Test 5
	Geometry and Measures 4	**Solving problems**	**Consolidation of KS3 work and start on KS4 work**	End of year test

© HarperCollins*Publishers* 2009

Matching charts

New Maths Frameworking Year 9 Scheme of Work

This matches the activities to the topics students will need to have covered to be able to tackle them. However, you need to think about the ability of your students and their stage of development. A good approach could be to use the activities a topic or two later to recall, revise and consolidate learning.

YEAR 9				Assessment
Term 1	**Algebra 1 & 2** Money matters 1: Pay (*) Rugby numbers (*) Revision planning (**)	**Number 1** Darts (*) Money matters 2: Tax and national insurance (**) Money matters 3: Loans and APR (**)		Test 1
	Algebra 3 Football (*) Bike race (**) Recipes (***)	**Geometry and Measures 1** Brick-laying patterns (*) Bridges (**)	**Statistics 1** Wales (*) Deliveries (*) Water (*)	Test 2
Term 2	**Geometry and Measures 2** Paving (*) Safe flying over the UK (*) Tile that wall (**)	**Number 2** Money matters 4: Savings and AER (**) Money matters 5: Mortgages (**)		Test 3
	Algebra 4 Time zones (**) Alcohol (***)	**Statistics 2** Endangered species (*) Follow that car (*) Stickers (**)	**Geometry and Measures 3** Join a group (*) Saving energy (***) Turn up the volume (***)	Test 4
Term 3	**Statistics 3** Shuffleboard (**) Body mass index (**)	**Statistics 4** Stopping distances (***) Climate change (***)	**Algebra 5** At the gym (**) Timetables (***)	Test 5
	Geometry and Measures 4 Green travel (**) Venting gas appliances (***) Planning a bedroom (***)	**Solving problems** Garden designer (***) Give us a job (***)	**Consolidation of KS3 work and start on KS4 work** Growing, growing, grown... (***) Populations (***)	End of year test

Matching charts

Framework matching chart

This matches the activities to the strands of the Framework for secondary mathematics, the APP criteria they could provide evidence for and lists the mathematical concepts that underpin them.

Activity	Stars	Framework strands	APP Criteria	Underpinning maths techniques needed
Timetables	3	Algebra, Mathematical processes and applications	Algebra, Using and applying mathematics	reading and interpreting timetables; calculating with time
Stopping distances	3	Algebra, Number	Algebra, Calculating	distance, time, speed; drawing and interpretation of graphs; conversion between linear metric and imperial units; probability
Football	1	Algebra, Number, Mathematical processes and applications	Algebra, Calculating, Using and applying mathematics	basic numeracy; negative numbers; powers; basic algebra
Brick-laying patterns	1	Geometry and measures	Shape, space and measures	symmetry
Bridges	2	Geometry and measures, Mathematical processes and applications	Shape, space and measures, Using and applying mathematics	basic number work
Paving	1	Geometry and measures, Mathematical processes and applications	Shape, space and measures, Using and applying mathematics	scale drawing; tessellations area; money problems in context
Safe flying over the UK	1	Geometry and measures, Mathematical processes and applications	Shape, space and measures, Using and applying mathematics	eight-point compass directions; three-figure bearings; multiplication and division by powers of 10
Garden designer	3	Geometry and measures, Mathematical processes and applications	Shape, space and measures, Using and applying mathematics	scale drawing; measuring; plan views
Planning a bedroom	3	Geometry and measures, Mathematical processes and applications	Shape, space and measures, Using and applying mathematics	scale drawing; measuring
Tile that wall	2	Geometry and measures, Mathematical processes and applications	Shape, space and measures, Using and applying mathematics	reflection, rotation, translation; symmetry; tessellations
Turn up the volume	3	Geometry and measures, Mathematical processes and applications	Shape, space and measures, Using and applying mathematics	volume of a cuboid; units of volume; estimation
Venting gas appliances	3	Geometry and measures, Mathematical processes and applications	Shape, space and measures, Using and applying mathematics	basic numeracy; scale drawing; estimation; reading tables and drawings.; ratio; gradient (optional)
Saving energy	3	Mathematical processes and applications	Using and applying mathematics	fractions; money calculations; estimation; area
Darts	1	Number	Calculating	multiplication by 2 and by 3; addition of three numbers, each up to 60

Matching charts

Money matters 1: Pay	1	Number	Calculating	basic numeracy; fractions and decimals
Money matters 2: Tax and national insurance	2	Number	Calculating	basic numeracy; percentages
Time zones	2	Number	Calculating	clock times; addition of times; subtraction of times
Join a group	1	Number, Geometry and measures, Mathematical processes and applications	Numbers and the number system, Shape, space and measures, Using and applying mathematics	multiples and factors; prime numbers; scale drawing
Deliveries	1	Number, Mathematical processes and applications	Calculating, Using and applying mathematics	measures; money; time; extracting information from tables, diagrams and charts; collecting and recording data; organising and representing information in different ways
Endangered species	1	Number, Mathematical processes and applications	Numbers and the number system, Using and applying mathematics	measures; extracting information from tables, diagrams and charts; collect and record data and organise and represent information in different ways
Revision planning	2	Number, Mathematical processes and applications	Calculating, Using and applying mathematics	time; reasoning; planning
Rugby numbers	1	Number, Mathematical processes and applications	Numbers and the number system, Using and applying mathematics	recognising and extending number patterns sequences
Give us a job	3	Number, Mathematical processes and applications	Calculating, Using and applying mathematics	calculations involving time and money; approximation and estimation; using a calculator to find percentages
Green travel	2	Number, Mathematical processes and applications	Calculating, Using and applying mathematics	estimation and rounding; scales on maps
Money matters 3: Loans and APR	2	Number, Mathematical processes and applications	Calculating, Using and applying mathematics	percentage of a quantity; understanding of annual percentage rate (APR)
Money matters 4: Savings and AER	2	Number, Mathematical processes and applications	Calculating, Using and applying mathematics	percentage of a quantity; understanding of annual equivalent rate (AER)
Money matters 5: Mortgages	2	Number, Mathematical processes and applications	Calculating, Using and applying mathematics	percentage of a quantity; understanding of annual equivalent rate (AER)
Recipes	3	Number, Mathematical processes and applications	Numbers and the number system, Using and applying mathematics	scaling quantities; using proportions; costing items; finding best value
Alcohol	3	Number, Mathematical processes and applications	Calculating, Using and applying mathematics	percentages; metric units; imperial units; decimals; estimation

© HarperCollins*Publishers* 2009

Matching charts

Bike race	2	Number, Mathematical processes and applications	Calculating, Using and applying mathematics	working with decimals to 3 decimal places; interpreting data presented in tables; selecting appropriate forms of presentation; speed
Growing, growing, grown…	3	Number, Mathematical processes and applications	Calculating, Using and applying mathematics	square numbers; powers; estimation; fractions
At the gym	2	Statistics, Mathematical processes and applications	Handling data, Using and applying mathematics	reading scales; reading graphs; estimation; metric units
Shuffleboard	2	Statistics, Mathematical processes and applications	Handling data, Using and applying mathematics	basic numeracy; negative numbers; stem-and-leaf diagram; averages of discrete data; mean of a grouped table; range; comparison of distributions using one measure of location and one measure of spread
Stickers	2	Statistics, Mathematical processes and applications	Handling data, Using and applying mathematics	experimental probability
Wales	1	Statistics, Mathematical processes and applications	Handling data, Using and applying mathematics	percentages; proportions; tally charts; bar charts; probability; eight-point compass; three-figure bearings
Body mass index	2	Statistics, Mathematical processes and applications	Handling data, Using and applying mathematics	using formulae; trial and improvement; rounding results of calculations; choosing appropriate tables or graphs to represent data; converting imperial units
Climate change	3	Statistics, Mathematical processes and applications	Handling data, Using and applying mathematics	interpreting graphs; time series graphs; percentages; fractions; number work
Follow that car	1	Statistics, Mathematical processes and applications	Handling data, Using and applying mathematics	extracting information from a variety of sources; collecting data through a survey; choosing the most appropriate way to present data
Populations	3	Statistics, Mathematical processes and applications	Handling data, Using and applying mathematics	carry out calculations in practical contexts; use equations; know how to choose a suitable format and scale to fit data
Water	1	Statistics, Number, Geometry and measures	Handling data, Calculating, Shape, space and measures	basic numeracy; estimation; reading pie charts; percentages; metric units

Functional Skills Checklist

Representing

- I can recognise that a real-life problem can be solved, using appropriate mathematics. ☐
- I can decide how to show the initial problem, using mathematical symbols. ☐
- I can decide which methods to use to make progress with the solution. ☐
- I can decide how to represent the problem to make it easier to solve using mathematics. ☐

Analysing

- I can use appropriate mathematical procedures. ☐
- I can analyse a pattern or a relationship, using appropriate techniques. ☐
- I can establish a pattern or relationship and then change the variables to see how this changes the results. ☐
- I can find a result or solution to the original problem. ☐

Interpreting

- I can interpret results and solutions and make a generalisation about them. ☐
- I can test generalisations and draw conclusions from the mathematical analysis. ☐
- I can check that a conclusion is appropriate and accurate in the context of the original problem. ☐
- I can give a conclusion or answer to the original problem, using language and forms of presentation that make sense to a wider population. ☐

Performing

- I can use mathematical skills and knowledge to make progress on a real-life problem, even if the situation described is not within a familiar context. ☐
- I can use mathematical skills and knowledge to make progress on a problem, even if it does not use a routine mathematical procedure. ☐
- I can analyse the situation or problem and decide which is the appropriate mathematical method needed to tackle it. ☐
- I can use a range of mathematics to find solutions. ☐
- I can check work and methods when tackling a problem and decide if a different approach may be more effective. ☐
- I can give a solution to a practical problem, even if the problem is not within a familiar context, and make sure the solution is presented in a clear and understandable way. ☐
- I can draw a conclusion from working and provide a mathematical justification for this conclusion. ☐

Acknowledgements

The publishers wish to thank the following for permission to reproduce photographs:

Cover image © Bob Battersby, BDI Images

The publishers wish to thank the following for permission to reproduce data: page 79 B&Q www.diy.com, pages 106–107 www.nationalrail.co.uk, page 109 Eurostar www.eurostar.com, pages 128–129 DVLA www.dvla.gov.uk, pages 135–138 Swiss Timing Ltd www.swiss-timing.com, page 153 DEFRA www.defra.gov.uk, pages 165–169 CIA www.cia.gov

Every effort has been made to trace copyright holders and to obtain their permission for the use of copyright material. The authors and publishers will gladly receive any information allowing them to rectify any error or omission at the first opportunity.